50
WAYS TO
GET
HIRED

50
WAYS TO
GET
HIRED

☆

MAX MESSMER

WILLIAM MORROW AND COMPANY, INC.
New York

It is the policy of William Morrow and Company, Inc., and its imprints and affiliates, recognizing the importance of preserving what has been written, to print the books we publish on acid-free paper, and we exert our best efforts to that end.

Library of Congress Cataloging-in-Publication Data

Messmer, Max, 1946–
    50 ways to get hired / by Max Messmer.
        p.   cm.
    ISBN 0-688-11566-7
    1. Job hunting.   2. Employment interviewing.
3. Vocational guidance.   I. Title.   II. Title: Fifty ways
to get hired.
HF5382.7.M47   1994
650.14—dc20   94-7520
                                                            CIP

Printed in the United States of America

        3   4   5   6   7   8   9   10

BOOK DESIGN BY MICHAEL MENDELSOHN/
MM DESIGN 2000, INC.

For my wife, Marcia,
my sons, Michael and Matthew,
and my mother, who have provided
love and support in many more than
"50 ways."

ACKNOWLEDGMENTS

50 Ways to Get Hired could not have been produced without a number of people who assisted with research and provided invaluable advice. I want to thank Barry Tarshis and John Boswell as well as members of the corporate communications staff of Robert Half International Inc., including Lynn Taylor, Steve Pehanich, and Annette Mowinckle for their excellent input. And a very special thanks to my friend and constant source of encouragement and support, Robert Half. Mr. Half began in 1948 authoring numerous highly acclaimed books and publications to assist employers in their hiring practices and candidates in their job searches. His widely read insights into these subjects remain an inspiration.

CONTENTS

PART I

ESSENTIALS

Nine things to think
about or do before you
do or think about
anything else

☆

1

ADAPT

I F I WERE TO BEGIN THIS BOOK by trying to convince you that the opportunities for finding good jobs are greater today than they have ever been and that there is a simple formula you can follow that will enable you to capitalize on these opportunities, I don't think you would find me especially credible.

The reason, of course, is that the job market today, as everyone knows, is tougher and more competitive than it has ever been. And even in a booming economy, where jobs are plentiful, I would not want to create the impression that finding and getting hired for a good job is a formulaic, by-the-numbers process, like building a model airplane or preparing a meal. It's not; nor has it ever been.

Having said this, let me add quickly that I am not nearly as pessimistic about the job market in the mid-1990s as a lot of people seem to be. Otherwise, I would not have written this book.

I am certainly aware—because of the business my company is in—of what has been happening in the job market over the past twenty years in America. And I'm well aware of all the jobs that have been eliminated by major corporations.

But I also know from firsthand experience that at the same time millions of jobs have disappeared, millions of others have been created. These are not "traditional" jobs in the normal sense of the term, which is to say that the job descriptions do not always lend themselves to traditional corporation classifications. More important, though, the chief source of these jobs is no longer major corporations, but small to mid-sized companies. Indeed, most new jobs being created in the United States are being created by businesses with fewer than twenty people.

And what do these changes mean to you, as someone now looking for a job? Simply this. You have to adapt. You need to bring to any job search undertaken today a mind set and a strategy that take into account the profound changes that have been taking place in the American workplace over the past twenty years. You can still prevail—but only if you play the game according to a new set of rules.

How much you have to adapt depends on you and what you are looking for. If you are fortunate, you can adapt to the changing job market in minor ways: by being flexible when it comes to the specifics of each opportunity—location, size of company, benefits package, and so forth.

It's possible, though, that you may have to make more fundamental changes. If you live in a region that has been hard hit by the economy, you may have to choose between changing careers entirely or moving to another part of the country. If you have spent nearly all your career in a field in which jobs are shrinking—banking, for instance—you may have to redirect your career goals to fields in which opportunities are growing: health care, perhaps, or education. This means, in turn, that you have to plan your next career move in a series of steps, rather than through a single job switch.

Finally, it might well be to your advantage to redefine your basic career goals and even rethink your definition of what it means to be "employed." Your next "job" may, in fact, be two or three jobs—each with a different company. And even though you may never have thought of yourself as an entrepreneur, you may well discover that running your own business is the best—and maybe *only*—way you're going to do what you do best and earn the kind of money you need to support the lifestyle you desire.

These choices are not easy, and I am not going to patronize you by reminding you of how "fortunate" you are to have so many "opportunities" before you. Clearly, though, the ground rules have changed, and the race in today's job market is not only geared to the swift or the persistent or even the most capable. It is geared to the resourceful, the opportunistic, and the courageous.

TAKE CHARGE

I F YOU WERE TO GO THROUGH the Career Management Seminar developed by Mary Lindley Burton and Richard Wedemeyer for the Harvard Business School Club of New York, the first piece of advice you would get is to appoint yourself the CEO of your job search. I can think of no single piece of job-hunting advice more valuable or more important to follow.

The rationale behind envisioning yourself as the

chief executive officer of your job search is twofold.

In the first place, there are genuine parallels between the types of decisions you need to make as the CEO of a company and the decisions you need to make as the CEO of your job search. In both instances, you are obliged to create and execute a plan, to marshal resources, to understand—and adjust to—changing market conditions. You also need to make tough decisions on the basis of inconclusive and sometimes conflicting data.

Equally important, though, is the fact that by envisioning yourself as the CEO of your job search, you establish the kind of mind-set a job search needs: proactive and self-directed.

The important and far-reaching implications of this principle cannot be overstated, and there is no way I can overemphasize how much impact a "being-in-control" mind-set can have on every aspect of your search. You can't control everything that has a bearing on your job search, of course—least of all, factors like the economy, industry trends, and the hiring policies of the companies you approach. What you *can* control, though, are the decisions you make in response to these factors—the job targets you set, the strategies you adopt, the daily routine you follow, and the skills you develop to make you a stronger candidate.

Don't shy away from this control. Psychologists have demonstrated in study after study a direct correlation between the emotional effects of stress and the degree to which you feel a sense of control over what is happening around you. A job search, even under the best of circumstances, is an emotional roller-coaster ride. The ride is a lot smoother when you are at the controls.

GET YOUR FINANCES IN ORDER

THE CHIEF SOURCE OF STRESS in most job searches—and the main reason job hunters make decisions they later regret—is financial pressure and the anxiety that accompanies it. The pressure is real; the anxiety is understandable.

Unless you are independently wealthy, it is next to impossible to escape the financial pressure that comes with the territory when you are out of work. But there are a few basic things you can do to minimize the day-to-day stress that financial insecurity can bring.

1. Make the Best Severance Deal Possible Unless you have a contract that says otherwise, severance is totally at the discretion of your employer, but this doesn't mean that you should view severance as a "gift." And it doesn't mean that you shouldn't try to negotiate for more than what has been offered.

The key to getting the most out of your severance package (assuming you still have time to do so) is to cite specific circumstances (other than the fact that you have to keep up payments on your new car) that entitle you to more severance than others in your position have received. Such circumstances might include having recently relocated in order to take the job you are now losing.

Even when it comes to traditional perks that normally become history as soon as you are dismissed—

industry-group and trade-organization memberships, for instance—you sometimes have room to negotiate. It may be possible to buy the company car or to take over the payments. It may also be possible to extend certain club memberships, at least until the annual membership fee comes due again. The point is, you'll never get what you don't ask for.

Medical benefits are different. Your former company, as of this writing, is legally bound to give you medical coverage for eighteen months following a layoff, but is not legally bound to pay for it. In a typical severance package, the company may pay for medical benefits for a limited period after which, you will be expected to pick up the expenses until you get a new job or until the eighteen months are up.

Most likely, it will be less expensive to keep your existing coverage than to take out a policy on your own, but do some comparison shopping all the same. Less expensive coverage might be available through a professional group or through your spouse's company. It may also be to your advantage—and you have to weigh this option very carefully—to drop the less essential parts of the coverage, depending on your needs and your cash-flow projections.

2. Sit Down with a Financial Planner One of your first priorities when you lose a job is to meet with someone who can help you put together a financial plan and a monthly budget designed to keep your head above water until you find another job. Not surprisingly, the toughest part about devising such a plan is estimating how long you expect to be out of work. A basic rule of thumb is to figure six months —at the very least—for any mid-level management position or higher. I would figure nine months.

Financial planners, remember, are not alchemists. They can't *create* money for you. They simply tell you how to manage the money you currently have and can count on in the months ahead through severance, unemployment compensation, your savings, temporary work, and other sources. A good planner will help you prioritize your expenses and should be able to give you a reasonable idea of what changes, if any, you need to make in your lifestyle if you want to stay within your budget.

3. Talk with Your Creditors Don't wait until you begin to fall behind in your monthly payments before you explain to your creditors *why* you're behind. Talk with your creditors early on. See if you can spread payments out over a longer time, thereby reducing your monthly expenditures.

4. Involve the Family The financial planning you do when you are out of work should be a family affair. Children old enough to work should be strongly urged to find part-time work. College-age children who've been receiving allowances should be expected to cut back or earn money on their own.

FINDING THE GOLDEN MEAN
The Tricky Basics of Job Targeting

WELL-DEFINED AND INTELLIGENTLY THOUGHT-OUT JOB TARGETS have always been the cornerstones of a successful job search. Without them, your job search will lack focus and direction. The quickest way to talk yourself *out* of a job offer is to confess to the person interviewing you that you are "open to a lot of possibilities."

Now for the fine print.

Figuring out what you would like to do—and are best equipped to do—in your next job is only one side of the job-targeting coin. You also need to determine how realistic those targets are. That's not easy to do, for there are many factors you have to consider, chief among them the following:

- The job opportunities that currently exist in the particular field or position you have targeted.
- The degree to which your professional experience, education, and skills match the generally recognized requirements for that position.
- The extent and caliber of the competition: how many other people with similar skills and similar backgrounds are competing for the same job.
- Your own personal requirements: the amount of money you need to live on, how flexible you can be with respect to relocation, etc.

There are no shortcuts to working your way through these factors. And because the answers to some of the questions you need to ask yourself may not be apparent, you may have to do some research. Begin by talking with as many people in the field as you can. Follow the classifieds to see if there are enough positions being advertised that you would like to explore. Try to meet recruiters or other people who have their ears to the track and can tell you about the hiring trends in a particular field. Read as much as you can.

If you talk with enough people and do your homework diligently, you should be able to gain a rough idea of how realistic your targets are, at which time the next questions you need to answer are: How committed are you to that target? How much does it mean to you? How hard are you willing to work? What sacrifices are you willing to make to reach your target?

Only you can answer these questions, but here are some suggestions to bear in mind while you are trying to answer them.

1. Don't be afraid to aim high, no matter what anyone tells you. Disappointing as it may be to fall short of a goal you've set, it is far worse to go through life haunted by the suspicion that you could have achieved much more, if only you had aimed higher.

2. Once you have decided to pursue a particular job target, give yourself every opportunity to be successful. Find out as much as you can—and as early as you can—about what it takes to be successful in the field and what specific skills and attributes the people doing the hiring are looking for. Talk to and associate with as many people in the field as you can. Read industry periodicals. Attend classes and lectures. Constantly strive to develop and improve upon the skills that underlie success in that field. In other words, don't wait for the opportunity to arise *before* you prepare. Be sufficiently prepared so that when an opportunity presents itself, you will be able to capitalize on it.

3. Be prepared to accept the possibility that, for whatever reason, you may have to scale back or

modify your job targets—not because there is anything wrong with you, but simply because market conditions dictate these moves.

It is never easy to determine when you need to scale back or modify a target, and it is even harder to determine when it is in your best interests to give up on the target altogether. The main thing is to do your best to keep your ego out of the process—no mean trick. Try to get some distance. Don't hang in there simply for the sake of hanging in there. Try not to get so caught up in the challenge and struggle of the search that you lose sight of what you're trying to find.

SOME THINGS YOU NEED TO BECOME EFFICIENT

I T HAS BEEN SAID BEFORE BUT IT BEARS REPEATING: Looking for a job is a full-time job. And as with any job, how efficiently you operate will go a long way to determine how effectively you perform.

Efficiency begins with having a well-organized base of operations. If outplacement is part of your severance package, you should probably take advantage of it. Just keep in mind that in a typical outplacement arrangement, you share office space with others, and you don't always have access to the office during the evening or on weekends. And while you

have secretarial and other kinds of support in a outplacement arrangement, you can't always operate according to *your* timetable.

All of which is another way of saying that even
with an outplacement arrangement, you should still
set up some sort of a base in your house or apart-
ment.

You don't need much space or equipment to
operate efficiently: a desk or table, a phone, good
lighting, enough room to sort out papers and to keep
your files well organized, and—not to be underval-
ued—a comfortable, supportive chair.

Privacy is essential. You need a place where you
can concentrate and where you can talk on the
phone without having to worry about the people
around you making noise.

Ideally, too, the environment should be reasonably cheery. You are going to be spending a good
deal of time in your home-office; do your best to
make your surroundings pleasant. Given a choice
between a small corner of a sunny bedroom or a
large, dank room above a garage, think small.

Beyond these basics, a number of items or pieces
of equipment could make things easier as you pro-
ceed in your job search. All require an investment,
and you will need to determine on an item-by-item
basis if the productivity you gain is worth the investment.

Personalized Stationery Get it in two sizes: 8½
by 11 inches for cover letters and general mailing;
smaller, monarch size for personal letters. Spend a
little extra to get a quality bond, but avoid anything
fussy or overtextured. If possible, get someone familiar with graphic design to select the typeface and

layout of the page. Otherwise, go through all the correspondence you receive, find a design and typeface that you like, and ask a printer or design studio to replicate it.

Answering Machine The telephone is the lifeline of a job search, and there is no excuse in this age of inexpensive answering machines and voice mail to miss out on an opportunity because you didn't get the message.

You have three choices: an answering service in which someone actually answers the phone and takes your messages; voice mail; or a telephone answering machine.

Answering machines are the best option for most people. Answering machines may be more expensive in the short term than monthly answering services or voice mail, but they'll save you money in the long run; and they have become so commonplace that hardly anyone objects any longer to leaving messages.

When you're shopping for an answering machine, make sure it has a remote capability, and when you set up your new machine spend some time on the recording you make. Keep your outgoing message simple, direct, and upbeat. Stay away from gimmicky openings (no music, please). Once you've recorded the message, ask friends to call, to listen, and to give you their reaction to your voice. Keep working on the message until you get an answer that makes you sound professional and upbeat.

One final note about phones: If you expect to be spending more than an hour or two each day on the phone, buy a headset. Headsets are not expensive, and they let you work with your hands without having to keep the handset tucked between your ear and shoulder.

Second Phone Line If you are working at home and will be sharing the phone with a roommate or with family members, consider installing a second telephone line—or, at the very least, a Call Waiting system. You will need one or the other to avoid the tension that can arise when you're waiting for a call and somebody else is on the phone.

While we're on the subject, make sure you set up a systematic way of handling messages. If someone other than you—a roommate, spouse, your children—will be answering the phone at times, make sure there is a pad and pen near the phone, and devise a system for writing down names and numbers. I shudder to think of the number of job opportunities that are lost because messages never get delivered or get delivered too late.

Facsimile Machine You can buy a no-frills facsimile machine or fax modem (assuming you have a computer) today for about two hundred and fifty dollars, and if you are looking for a job in middle management or above, the investment is worth it. The convenience of it notwithstanding, having your own facsimile capability reflects a seriousness of purpose that in certain situations and with some employers could give you an edge over other candidates.

If you don't want to *buy* a facsimile machine or fax modem, set up an arrangement either with someone who has one or with one of the commercial centers that offer copying, faxing, and other services for a fee.

Home Computer If this book were being written as recently as five years ago, I might not have recommended to job hunters who didn't own or have access to a computer that they go out and buy one, especially if they had never worked with a computer before.

I feel differently today, however—and for a variety of reasons.

The main advantage to having access to (and being able to use) a computer in your job search is that it vastly enhances your productivity. Instead of having to type a new letter (or getting someone to type it for you) each time you need to respond to an ad or write a thank-you note, you simply call up to the screen letters you've already written and, with minor edits, generate a new letter in a matter of moments.

What's more, the simple calendar and database programs that come packaged with most computers can help you stay organized and better focused. And if you have a modem, you can gain access (for a small on-line fee) to on-line business lists, without having to leave your office.

Computers today are not nearly as expensive as they once were. You can now buy a highly serviceable—if slightly less than state-of-the-art—computer, along with a decent, letter-quality printer and some basic software for less than a thousand dollars—even less if you buy used equipment. This is not an insignificant sum for someone out of work, but it's not an outrageous amount, either—not when you consider what it adds to your overall job search productivity.

Assuming you can handle the expense of a computer, the question for those not already computer literate becomes whether you want to introduce at this stage of your life a possible source of frustration: learning how to use the thing.

I say, yes. Most software programs today—particularly those you will be using in your job search— are easier than ever to learn. More important, familiarity with computers is something virtually every professional, at any level, should have.

A final word of advice: Keep things simple. You do not need an elaborate system or expensive software to handle the most important tasks in a job search. The least expensive machines are more than adequate to write letters and maintain simple databases.

GET TIME TO WORK IN YOUR FAVOR

ONE OF THE MANY IRONIES OF LOOKING FOR A JOB is that you frequently don't know what to do with the one thing you never seemed to have enough of when you were actually working. I'm talking about time.

The problem here is twofold. First of all, it has to do with the unstructured nature of job hunting; second, with the difficulty of a transition from the structure and the "never enough hours in the day" pressure of full-time employment to the unstructured "inactivity" of being out of a job.

The only truly effective way to counteract this all too common pitfall of job hunting is to create your own structure—that is, impose upon yourself a schedule that approximates the structure you would be working within if you were showing up to work each day at a full-time job. This means a "working day," with specific activities scheduled for specific times of the day.

The nature of your daily schedule and the time you allot to various tasks that make up the schedule will vary, of course, depending upon priorities—what is happening at any given time in a job search.

But even if you have nothing pressing—no interviews to get ready for, no job leads to follow-up on—scheduling becomes no less important. For there is *always* something you could be doing at any given time in a job search to improve your chance of getting hired.

That "something" might be reading the latest business publications in the library for new ideas about which fields offer hiring opportunities and which companies are expanding. It might be going through your college alumni magazines for names of people who might know of job leads. It might be taking a seminar that will teach you a skill that will make you a more attractive candidate.

Whatever it is, you need to make it a structured part of your schedule. Otherwise, you may never get around to doing it. Here are a few ideas on scheduling.

1. Develop a System Buy or create on your own some sort of calendar-planning system—one that enables you not only to list the tasks you want to accomplish on a daily and weekly basis but to prioritize those tasks as well. While you're at it, set up a filing system that makes it easy for you to compartmentalize the various components of your job search: one folder for job leads you're currently pursuing; another for letters; another for contacts, and so on.

2. Set Measurable Goals For every activity you schedule, set a goal—even if it's a small goal. If you plan to spend two hours in the library tomorrow morning researching companies you might approach, or if you intend to spend the better part of the morning making phone calls to expand your network of contacts, give yourself targets: no fewer than four companies, no fewer than six new contacts. You may not always achieve your goal, but the simple act of *setting* the goal will generally motivate you to accomplish more than you might otherwise have accomplished. And when you do, in fact, reach your goal, the feeling of accomplishment will carry over into other aspects of your job search.

3. Monitor Your Productivity Get into the habit at the end of each day of looking back and evaluating how productive you were that day, based on how closely you stuck to your schedule and how successful you were in achieving your goals. If you didn't stick to the schedule and were not able to achieve your goals, ask yourself why. Was it something that you could not have predicted or prevented—for example, a personal emergency? Or did you simply allow yourself to be distracted?

If distractions were indeed the culprit, don't beat yourself up. Try to figure out what specific distractions were to blame, and make a commitment not to allow the same distractions to interfere with your productivity on the following day.

DEVELOP A LONG-HAUL MENTALITY

L EARN PATIENCE.
Progress in a job search is not something you can readily measure on a day-to-day basis. It's not like losing weight, or increasing the number of push-ups you do each day. The day-to-day results in the typical job hunt are not usually apparent. Failure, in fact, is a fixed part of the script.

Consider this: A professional baseball player who fails to get a hit 70 percent of the time is still a good bet for the Hall of Fame, as long as he can maintain that "failure" rate for a dozen or so seasons. Direct-mail specialists are thrilled if 98 percent of the people they've written *don't* respond (which means, of course, that 2 percent *do* respond).

In a successful job search, the "failure" rate is likely to be very high. Until you are offered a job you feel good about accepting, most of the things you do—the calls you make, leads you follow, openings you get a crack at—are unlikely to produce the results you want.

Pace yourself. Being motivated and staying energized are critical. Putting unnecessary pressure on yourself and expecting the job search process to give you the same kind of feedback you were accustomed to when you were working is a recipe for frustration and disappointment.

It might help you to liken your job search to the challenge police detectives face when investigating a homicide. Homicide detectives know that most of the leads they follow aren't going to amount to anything, but they have no way of knowing ahead of time where any given lead will take them. Their job, in a sense, is not so much to "solve the crime"; that's the goal. It is to uncover and follow up on leads. Your *goal* in a job search is to get a good offer. Your *job* is to do what it takes to get that offer.

YOU CAN'T DO IT ALONE

THE DAY FRAN B. WAS HIRED by an electronics firm in northern California, she went out and bought two bottles of champagne.

She gave one bottle to the masseuse she'd been going to every other Saturday morning during her six-month job search (a massage, she says, was the one luxury she kept in her budget; besides, the masseuse agreed to lower her fees until Fran had a new job). She gave the other bottle to the woman who ran the reference department of her local library.

Why the librarian? Because the librarian had been a godsend throughout Fran's job search. Her knowledge of lists and directories had saved Fran countless hours of tedious research. On several occasions, she had bent the rules, allowing Fran to take reference directories home at night, with the assurance that everything would be returned early the next morning.

People like the librarian who was so helpful to Fran play an important and not always appreciated role in a successful job search. They are not really part of your professional network—that is, you do not rely on them for names or job leads or insights into the job market. Their role is to give you support in smaller ways and to be there for you on a more or less constant basis.

The people I'm referring to here are your sounding boards, your reality checks, your mood picker-uppers. They help with little things—letting you use the copying machine in their office; watching one of your kids on a day when you have an interview and the baby sitter calls up at the last minute to cancel.

I have observed many job hunters who have an uncanny ability to get help from these kinds of sources. These people share the following key characteristics:

1. They are not embarrassed to ask for the help they need.
2. The help they ask for does not create undue pressure or inconvenience for the people called upon.
3. They never take the help they receive for granted. They show their gratitude in tangible ways.

Follow their example. Spend time in the beginning of your job search to think about the people you know. Pull them together, informally, into a team. Strive for balance. Choose your closest and most reliable friends for general support, but make sure there are two or three people, not necessarily your closest friends, whom you can use as sounding boards—people whose candor you can rely upon.

Once you have made your choices, get in touch with each person individually. Let each member of your team know the kind of help you're looking for, and ask them if they are willing to give you that help. If you sense hesitation, withdraw the request.

Forget the notion that you are "imposing" or "using" people. Most people are flattered when you seek their help or advice—as long as your requests are reasonable. One stylish woman I know was called recently by a friend who wanted to make the woman her official "job-wardrobe fashion consultant." Far from feeling put upon, the woman was delighted, and spent what she described as a very enjoyable two days helping her friend put together a job-search wardrobe.

There are lots of people out there who want to help you. Give them the chance.

COMIC RELIEF
Seven Ways to Keep Your Spirits Up— No Matter How Lousy Things Are Going

1. Don't Deprive Yourself Unnecessarily Being out of work usually obliges you to make certain sacrifices in your lifestyle, but don't overdo it. And whatever you do, avoid the "I have no right to enjoy myself" syndrome. As long as you can afford it and are focusing the bulk of daily energy on your job search, there is no reason to give up any of the activities that gave you pleasure while you were working full-time.

2. Do Things You Couldn't Do If You Were Working Remember all the things you used to wish you could do if only you weren't so busy at work, like spending more quality time with your kids, staying in closer touch with friends, listening to good music, or going for long walks or bike rides first thing in the morning. Involved as you are in your job search, try to work some pleasurable tasks into your daily routine. Busy as you are, remember that you are still in control of your time. Don't minimize the pleasures that come from no longer having a boss.

3. Get into Better Shape Try to work into your weekly routine some form of regular exercise, even if it's a thirty-minute walk three times a week. The benefits of exercise take on added importance when you're under the stress of job hunting. Getting into shape will help your appearance as well, which, in turn, will make you a more attractive candidate.

4. **Join a Support Group** In all likelihood, your community, church, synagogue, or professional association has organized a support group made up of people who, like you, are looking for work. As you might expect, the quality of the counseling programs offered by these groups varies enormously, but I have yet to meet anyone involved with such a group who didn't benefit from the involvement.

5. **Watch What You Feed Your Mind** Impose a limit on the amount of bad news you absorb each day. Spend as much time as you can around people who make you feel good, and as little time as possible with people who depress you.

Other suggestions:

- Read as many inspirational, self-help books as you can get your hands on. Type out the passages that make you feel better and paste them in visible places, like on your refrigerator door or above your computer screen.
- Buy or get from the library motivational tapes to play in your car, especially on your way to an interview.
- Go to a video store and buy tapes of your four or five favorite comedies. Play them whenever you feel yourself getting depressed.
- Instead of the murders and fires you see on late-night news, make reruns of *Cheers* or M*A*S*H the last thing you watch before going to sleep.
- Keep humorous books on your bedside table.
- Spend as much time as you can with upbeat people, and do your best to avoid people

who want to burden you excessively with *their* problems.

6. **Develop New Skills and Interests** The best way to keep your mind off problems is to find something new and interesting to occupy your thoughts. Find a volunteer organization (see page 87). Look into adult education programs in your community. They're inexpensive and an excellent way to get you involved in subjects—art, music, history, a foreign language—that can make your life richer, more interesting, and more fulfilling.

7. **Learn to Fake It** Even if you're *not* feeling positive or optimistic, do your best to act as though you *were*, particularly when you're talking to anybody who could prove helpful to you in your job search. Limit the self-commiserating you do to private moments— when you're alone or with people you can count on to give you love and support.

PART II

MARKETING YOURSELF
Ten Ways to Make Yourself More Marketable

☆

RECOGNIZE THE DIFFERENCE BETWEEN SELF-WORTH AND MARKET VALUE

HOW MARKETABLE ARE YOU?

This question strikes some people as being crass and dehumanizing. Yet, it is a question you must ask yourself early on in your job search and one you must keep asking yourself over and over as your job search progresses.

Some people confuse market value with self-worth. There's a big difference. Self-worth has to do with how much you value yourself as an individual, quite apart from the money you earn and what you do for a living.

Market value applies *solely* to how much demand there is in the marketplace for your particular mix of experience, skills, and personal attributes. Market value relates to the kinds of jobs you can reasonably expect to be in the running for, and what you can reasonably expect to be paid.

Self-worth is obviously an important component in a job search, but you make a serious tactical error when you fail to distinguish between the person you look at in the mirror each day and the person would-be employers see when they look at your résumé or talk with you during an interview.

You make an equally serious tactical error when you fail to take into account how widely your market value can vary from situation to situation and from one month to the next—depending on your background, what new skills you have developed, or what additional experience you have been able to add to your résumé.

Here is a brief look at some of the factors that help to determine your market value.

Professional Background and Experience This category relates to jobs you have actually held at various stages of your career and, in particular, the most recent of these jobs. Most important here, of course, are the specific tasks you performed and responsibilities you held in these jobs. Everything else being equal, your professional background and experience—what you have actually done—has more bearing on your market value than any other element in this mix.

Accomplishments Those things in previous jobs that produced tangible results are your accomplishments: money you saved or earned for your employers; productivity that increased because of ideas you introduced. Accomplishments contribute significantly to your market value but—and this is important—only insofar as those accomplishments relate to the needs of a prospective employer.

Credentials Specific degrees or licenses that verify your having completed a course of study, gone through a certain type of training, or passed a standardized test—these are your credentials. The market value of credentials varies from profession to profession, from industry to industry, and, in some cases, from company to company.

Connections "Who you know" plays a much more important role in market value than many people think, albeit a more important role in certain fields and professions than in others. We know from our experience with financial professionals, for instance, that accountants who can attract clients have a decided edge over those who can't. It is not by accident that no matter how tight the economy is, people who have occupied high places in government seldom have to look very hard to find companies eager for their services.

Hard Skills The specific things you know how to do are labeled *hard skills*. The machines you can operate, the systems you know, your ability to write, edit, and speak foreign languages—these are all examples of hard skills. Here again, the market value of hard skills varies according to the position you're trying to fill. But they are particularly important for entry-level candidates who do not have specific job targets.

Personal Attributes All the non-job-related things that distinguish you as an individual from other people constitute your personal attributes: your appearance, personality, work habits, and ambition. Personal attributes obviously go a long way in determining how effective you are once you get a job, and they can be a factor in how well you come across during a job interview. In general, though, your personal attributes in and of themselves do not contribute to your *market value*. They serve mainly to *enhance* your value once the other components have clicked in.

*   *   *

What does all this mean?

Simply this: Do your best to arrive at and maintain a reasonably objective sense of your own market value, particularly with respect to jobs you have targeted. More important, try to improve yourself in those areas that will have the most immediate impact on your market value.

IDENTIFY YOUR UNIQUE SELLING PROPOSITION

S IMPLY BEING "GOOD" AT WHAT YOU DO is no longer enough to get you hired for most jobs today.

It isn't enough, in other words, to be a capable and experienced engineer, accountant, salesperson, nutritionist, or computer programmer. You need what marketing specialists like to call USP—a Unique Selling Proposition. You need to be an engineer, accountant, salesperson, nutritionist, or computer programmer who has an exceptional quality that goes beyond the basic qualifications for the job—something that visibly sets you apart from other candidates.

Your USP could be any number of things.

It might be the fact that you speak three or four languages, that you communicate exceptionally well, that you're a computer whiz familiar with all the major software programs, or that you are someone who digs your teeth into everything you do and won't let go until the task is completed.

It might be your leadership skills—your ability to motivate the people who work for you, or your ability to sweat the details that other people let slip through the cracks.

Whatever it is, you need to identify it and build your marketing campaign around it. You need to communicate your USP in your cover letters and in every interview. More than simply selling *yourself*, you need to sell your USP.

If the idea of looking at yourself and what makes you special and unique seems overwhelming to you, here are a few suggestions.

1. Pretend you have been asked to write a recommendation for yourself and that you *must* include in that recommendation no fewer than five of your chief assets—five strong reasons why somebody would want to hire you. Once you have written down these assets, pick the strongest one and see if you can pinpoint accomplishments or experiences in which that asset was instrumental to your success.

2. Go to people who know you well—family members, friends, former employers—and ask them to help you identify the one or more qualities that might set you apart from others competing for the job.

3. Don't equate the process of figuring out your USP with being "conceited" or "tooting your own horn." See it as an essential step in your job search—something you *must* do in order to remain competitive in a competitive marketplace.

12

YOUR APPEARANCE
Okay, You're Not Robert Redford or Michelle Pfeiffer, but ...

THE MAIN THING TO BEAR IN MIND about your appearance and how it affects your job search is this: What counts the most is not so much your physical characteristics, per se—how tall you are, how much you weigh, and so forth. What counts is the overall impression you convey by virtue of your appearance: how professional you look, and how much energy, enthusiasm, and confidence you generate. Equally important is how you carry yourself when you walk into a room, the firmness of your handshake, whether you look people in the eye when you talk to them. It all contributes.

You can go to any library or bookstore and find many books on how to dress and groom yourself so that you look your best in the eyes of would-be employers. Most of these books carry the same message: Dress conservatively. Blend in, don't stand out. Go easy on the cologne or perfume. In short, play it safe.

Rather than echo the advice offered in those books, let me emphasize a few of the points about appearance that don't always get the attention they deserve, based on what I see happening daily in the real world.

1. Don't Stint on Quality As long as you don't go overboard, spending extra money on your job-search wardrobe and appearance in general should not be viewed as an extravagance but as an investment, particularly if you are competing for jobs in mid- to senior management. If you need clothes and are on a tight budget, find a high-end consignment shop. Even with the cost of tailoring, you can still figure to save as much as 70 percent on most items you buy from such outlets.

2. **Make Sure Your Clothing Fits Well** The stress of being out of work induces some people to *put on* weight and causes others to *lose* weight. If your weight has changed significantly since your last clothing purchase, buy new clothes or have the clothes you already own altered.

3. **Feel Good About What You Wear** Regardless of how terrific other people insist you look in a particular outfit, be sure that you feel good about the way it looks and feels on you. If you're not accustomed to wearing business attire—and many young people aren't—get used to how it feels to be dressed in clothes you intend to wear during an interview by wearing that outfit for an hour or so when you're simply hanging around the house.

I heard a story not long ago about a young man who went on an interview and seemed so uncomfortable throughout that the interviewer finally asked him if anything was wrong. There was. The young man had borrowed a pair of his brother's shoes, which were so tight—a size and a half *smaller* than they should have been—they were literally biting into the poor candidate's feet.

4. **Don't Let Your Guard Down** Be as attentive to how you look and what you wear when you are

running around town doing errands as you are when you're meeting people. You never know whom you're going to run into (or who may take notice of you without your even being aware of it). Wherever you go, look neat and well groomed.

HONE YOUR COMPETITIVE EDGE

WHEN THE ART DIRECTOR of a now-defunct advertising agency in Boston found himself looking for a job a year ago, he discovered early on in his search that he had made a critical tactical mistake while he was still working. He had never gotten around to learning computer graphics. He'd always believed that the traditional way of doing page layouts—doing them manually—was the best way to do creative work.

Maybe he's right. I don't know that much about computer graphics. What I do know, however, is that the first thing most ad agencies ask graphic designers looking for a job these days is what desktop publishing programs they're familiar with. Lacking expertise in these programs, the art director was out of the running before he even entered the race.

You cannot expect to compete successfully in today's job market if your skills and knowledge have not kept pace with the changes and technological advancements that have taken place in your field.

So even before you set your sights on a specific job target, make sure your training and skills can match what other candidates are able to offer.

One piece of advice we give repeatedly to financial professionals we work with is that they become familiar with as many of the various spreadsheet and accounting software packages as possible. The issue is *not* whether they really need to know these programs to do a good job. The issue is how much these programs have become a fixed part of the job descriptions in so many companies.

Put yourself in the shoes of the person interviewing you. If you were the head of a small business in need of a controller, and you had narrowed down your list of candidates to two people, one of whom already knew how to work the accounting software your company was using, which of the two candidates would you be more likely to choose?

You may have some catching up to do. You might have to learn new skills, take courses, get some special training, attend seminars, or put yourself on a crash-course reading program.

At the very least, you should be reading the key trade journals in any field or industry in which you have established job targets and you should get hold of a college catalogue to see what specific courses college students training for your field are now being required to take. It is not enough to tell an interviewer that you're willing and able to *learn* a particular skill. In today's market, if you don't already *have* a skill that other candidates have, you won't even get a chance to interview.

The fact is, you have no choice. Sooner or later, if you want to compete on an equal footing with other candidates, you will have to develop the skills that have become basic requirements for the jobs you are seeking. The earlier in your job search you begin to catch up, the quicker you'll be able to even out the playing field.

TRANSFERRING SKILLS
How to Reposition Yourself Without Falling on Your Face

I N THE 1967 ROBERT ANDERSON play called *You Know I Can't Hear You When the Water's Running*, an actor wearing an outrageous toupee shows up at an audition determined to convince the producers that no matter what part might be available in the play, he can play it.

It's a very funny scene to watch onstage. It's not as funny when the scene is unwittingly played by job candidates insisting in their job interviews that they can do a particular job, but are unable to offer anything other than their insistence to substantiate their claim.

At issue here is an idea getting quite a bit of press these days. It's called *transferring skills*.

The notion behind transferring skills is simple. You look at the skills, experience, and training that enabled you to perform effectively in other jobs you have held, and you try to match those skills, experience, and training to the requirements of jobs in a different field.

The principle is sound—and certainly important if your previous jobs have been in an industry in which opportunities are dwindling. The problem, though, is that in a competitive market, you are frequently competing with candidates who, on paper at least, are qualified even without having to transfer skills or industries. In other words, the notion of "transferred skills" is not an easy sell to most employers.

I don't want to paint too bleak a picture. You need to be careful, though, that you don't fall into the trap of thinking that simply by word-smithing your résumé, you are going to make the transfer process work in your job search. You must be able to demonstrate specifically how the skills you put to use in your last job will make you effective and productive in your new job, should you be hired. More important, you need to turn the "disadvantage" into an "advantage"—that is, demonstrate that your skills and background, different though they may be from other candidates, bring added value to the new job.

Here's an example of what I mean. Several months ago, we worked with a small, highly entrepreneurial apparel company that was looking for a controller. The company's president emphasized that what he *didn't* want was someone who had spent nearly all of his or her career with a big CPA firm. He wanted somebody who could cope with the pressures typically found in smaller, more fluid environments.

As things turned out, the candidate who eventually got the job had spent the bulk of his career with a major firm. But he also had a wealth of experience with importing companies—experience that many other candidates didn't have.

The accountant's challenge was to convince the company's president that he could work effectively in a smaller environment—something he was able to do by pointing out that over the past few years, his former firm had restructured itself so that people worked in small, reasonably independent units. It helped, too, that the accountant came across during the interviews as someone who wasn't afraid to roll up his sleeves and do whatever needed to be done.

To repeat the key point: Being able to transfer your skills is more important in today's job market than ever before. Make sure, however, that you do three things: One, think out the process carefully before you go after any particular job; two, base your transfer strategy on what the new position requires, as opposed to what you can offer; and, three, be able to demonstrate—with past accomplishments—how your skills not only relate to the company's goals, but how your transferred skills can help the company to achieve those goals.

YOUR RÉSUMÉ
Just Do It

SOME PASSING THOUGHTS ABOUT RÉSUMÉS:

1. Your résumé, important as it is, is only one component of your job-search strategy, and there is a point at which the time and effort you spend on it become counterproductive. True, a badly

written résumé—that is, one that is illogically organized and written in garbled prose—can knock you out of the running. Beyond a certain point, though, how the résumé is *written* has little bearing on your chances of being interviewed or being hired. A résumé doesn't get you the job. It simply puts you in the running.

2. The process of putting together a strong résumé is as important as the résumé itself. So even if someone else is helping you put the résumé together, *you* need to do the bulk of the work, focusing in particular on which aspects of your background are likely to capture the interest of a would-be employer.

Do I mean to suggest by these two observations that your résumé is unimportant? Not at all. A good résumé is obviously important, and you can't expect to conduct a successful job search without one. What needs to be understood, though, is what makes a résumé "good."

Let me tell you what I look for, and what most employers look for in a résumé.

I look for a document that will tell me, in one or two pages, what specific business or professional experience a candidate has had, what the candidate has accomplished in his or her career, and what sort of training and education the person has had.

That's pretty much it.

Do I care about the way the résumé looks? Yes, but only to the extent that the résumé is neat, professional-looking, and easy to read. Do I pay attention to the writing style? Not really—not unless I find the résumé unusually difficult to wade through or overburdened with glitzy terms. Again, I am interested in what the résumé says about the candidate, and not how it says it.

There is a glut of books, articles, tapes, and software programs available today offering advice on how to write a winning résumé. Rather than reiterate the advice found in these publications, let me offer a few comments on some of the issues and questions that typically arise when you are putting together a résumé:

Length A standard résumé runs one page, but if you need an extra page to describe important aspects of your background, use it. Just make sure the added information is relevant.

Layout Keep the layout of your résumé simple and uncluttered. Use boldface or all caps for headings, but stick with one typeface, and make sure the left and right margins are at least one inch. The format I prefer is one in which the dates of employment are listed in a small column to the left of the page, and the job and description are placed in a second, much wider column.

A Career Objective Unless you are a recent high school or college graduate seeking an entry-level position, leave it out. If you want to mention your objective, do it in your cover letter and make sure the objective you state is tailored to the job you're seeking.

A Paragraph That Summarizes Your Background This is a good idea as long as the paragraph isn't loaded with generalities that can just as easily be said about thousands of other people. (Test: If the paragraph you've written could just as easily describe thousands of other people competing for the same position, rewrite it or leave it out.)

Preparing More Than One Résumé Tailoring a résumé to specific industries or to specific kinds of jobs is a good idea, and in the age of computers, it's easy to pull off. I know of successful job hunters who created new résumés almost on a company-by-company basis, and could produce a "new" résumé in a matter of minutes.

Personal Interests If you have room, include your personal interests—but with this caveat: Include only those interests that demonstrate skills and attributes that could affect job performance. Being an "excellent skier," as one résumé I read recently reported, is nice, but only if your career objective is to become a ski instructor. The fact that you run marathons, on the other hand, says something about your determination and self-discipline—attributes that many employers would probably care about.

Gaps in the Résumé Don't lie about them. If there are gaps in your career—for instance, you took off three or four years to raise your children—explain them in the cover letter.

16

DON'T HIDE YOUR LIGHT UNDER A BUSHEL

THERE IS ONE PIECE OF RÉSUMÉ ADVICE I consider so important, it deserves its own listing. What brings it to mind is a conversation I had with the daughter of a friend who had asked me to look over her résumé.

The young woman was a recent college graduate, so her résumé, predictably, did not go into great detail about her professional experience. It did, however, highlight some of her activities in college, one of the items on the résumé being: "Resident advisor: counseled group of freshmen students living in same dorm."

Mainly out of curiosity, I asked the young woman to tell me about that experience. She told me that being appointed a residence advisor was considered a major honor at the school and that there were more than seventy-five applicants for each position.

Really?

Her résumé *now* reads "Resident advisor: One out of a field of seventy-five applicants chosen to serve as counselor to freshmen students living in same dorm."

The lesson: Whenever you present your qualifications to anyone, whether in a résumé, letter, or in person, look for the light under the bushel—the specific element of that experience that shows you off to your best advantage.

17

HOW TO WRITE THE GREAT AMERICAN COVER LETTER

I WOULD BE LYING IF I TOLD YOU that I read every résumé that crossed my desk. But I have rarely *not* looked at a résumé that was accompanied by a solid, well-written cover letter. The lesson here: Learn how to write a strong letter.

A cover letter should be more than wrapping paper for your résumé. It should help to set you apart from other candidates. It should give the person reading it a *compelling reason* to want to see you.

If a cover letter is to meet this tall order, it must, above all, depict you as someone who has skills, knowledge, or attributes that could make a *tangible* contribution to the company you are approaching—based on that company's current needs.

Most cover letters I read do not do this. Most cover letters focus too much on what a candidate is *looking for* and not enough on what the candidate can *offer* the would-be employer. In job hunting, as in sales in general, your focus should be on the *benefit*, not the *feature*.

Here are some guidelines to keep in mind whenever you write cover letters:

- Use personalized letterhead stationery.
- Address the letter to a specific person, even if you have to make a dozen phone calls to get the name, the correct spelling, and the proper title.

If, regardless of what you've done, you cannot get the name and address, use a standard "To whom it may concern." It's not great, but it's safe.

- Avoid gimmicky openings. Not everyone would agree with me, but I don't consider it a good idea to begin a cover letter with the kind of jazzy opening you might use for a direct-mail piece. Yes, such openings attract attention, but more often than not, they seemed forced and insincere. You are better off letting the reader know, in the first paragraph, why you're writing and why it is in the reader's best interest to pay attention to what you're saying.

- Don't rehash your résumé. Focus instead on your USP (Unique Selling Position, see page 44) and on two or three qualities you want to emphasize about yourself. Try to connect those qualities to the key requirements of the job.

- Try to work into the letter information that reflects your knowledge of the company you are addressing, the industry, and any problems or issues that are relevant to them.

- Write the way you speak—more or less, anyway. Important as it is to honor the rules of standard English, it is just as important in cover letters to avoid stiff, bureaucratic jargon. Write to inform, not to impress. (Hint: If you are tempted to use a word in a letter that you would not be likely to use in person, replace it with a word that is more conversational.)

- Check and recheck every letter you send for typos, bad grammar, and spelling mistakes. Find somebody—a friend or spouse, for instance— who is good at proofreading, and have that person check everything you write. If you use a computer, consider buying a computerized spelling and grammar checker. These programs are not foolproof, but they catch the most obvious errors. Otherwise, keep a dictionary or usage primer handy.

It may not be fair, but usage and grammar mistakes in your letters frequently turn off a potential employer, regardless of your other qualifications. These errors could lead some people to conclude that if you weren't careful enough to avoid mistakes in your job search, you are likely to be careless when it comes to job performance.

DEVELOP A FIFTEEN-SECOND SALES PITCH

O VER AND OVER IN YOUR JOB SEARCH, you are going to be asked to perform a simple task: Explain in two or three sentences who you are, what you want, and why the person you're talking to should be interested in what you have to say. The sooner you prepare and commit to memory this brief but critical script, the better off you're going to be.

Here is a simple model to follow:

1. Identify who you are. ("My name is . . .")
2. Describe in one or two sentences, your profes-

sion, occupation, or background. ("I'm a human-resources professional with ten years of experience, mostly with large manufacturing companies.")

3. Spell out what you want from the person you're talking to. ("I'm looking to join a company that needs help in retraining its employees to meet the new demands of the marketplace.")

You can vary this basic pitch in any number of ways, depending on the situation, your audience, and what aspect of your background you want to highlight. The important thing is to be able to present this thumbnail picture clearly, smoothly, and with confidence.

DON'T POSITION YOURSELF AS A "BARGAIN"

IF YOU ARE SELLING CARS OR TELEVISION SETS, letting customers think they're getting a bargain is frequently a good way to make a sale. But it is not a smart move when you're looking to get hired for a good job. Here's why.

Even before the interviewing process begins, most employers have a general idea of the salary range they are able, and prepared, to pay for a particular position. That number is based on several factors. The most important factor, though, is the recognized market value for a particular job, given the duties and responsibilities it entails.

If the salary you are seeking far *exceeds* that market value, you will probably scare people off and knock yourself out of the running. You run a comparable risk, though, if the salary you are seeking falls well *below* what the company is prepared to pay. Far from viewing you as a "bargain," many would-be employers are likely to interpret lower salary demands as a sign that there is something wrong with you.

There's another dynamic working here as well. Hiring is a long and often expensive process. When a company makes a hiring decision, it wants to be as sure as it can that whoever it hires is not going to jump ship the moment a better offer comes along. Pricing yourself *below* market value could send a signal to a would-be employer that you view this job as only a stop-gap measure. It doesn't foster confidence.

PART III

GETTING INTO THE HUNT

Fifteen Ways to Drum Up Job Leads

☆

20

THE JOB YOU NEVER HEAR ABOUT IS THE JOB YOU'LL NEVER GET

WHEN JOB HUNTERS TELL ME ABOUT JOBS they "didn't get," they are usually referring to jobs they've heard about, applied for, and may even have been interviewed for.

There is, however, a much bigger category of jobs that you are not going to get. These are the jobs you never hear about.

What it all comes to in the end is this: In today's job market, regardless of who you are, you cannot afford to sit back and wait for opportunities to materialize, and you cannot afford to rely solely on conventional methods of generating job leads. Yes, conventional approaches—the want ads, recruiters, and so forth—are important, but you must look beyond these sources. You need to be aggressive, creative, and resourceful.

In the rest of this section, I will look into some of the specific techniques you can use to extend your job-lead reach. Some of these techniques may not apply directly to your situation, and your specific job-search strategy might be better served by one technique than another.

In any event, you should be prepared to use *all* the techniques I will describe. And I can't emphasize enough the importance of keeping your eyes and ears open at all times. You never know where, when, and how a job lead will materialize.

I heard recently about a computer systems specialist who, as he was leaving the unemployment office one afternoon, happened to notice someone painting a company's name on one of the office doors in the same building. He asked some questions, found out about the company and managed to set up an interview that led to a job. I know of countless other instances in which people were hired for jobs they first got wind of in a dizzying variety of serendipitous ways—everything from overheard comments on elevators to casual conversations with strangers in a movie line.

Remember, all you need is *one* lead that ultimately leads to a job offer. Keep in mind, as you read through the rest of this section, that you will never be offered a job you never hear about.

21

DIG WITH EFFICIENCY

IT IS ONE THING TO PULL TOGETHER, and continually add to, a list of companies that might hire you. It is another thing to manage this aspect of your job search efficiently and strategically.

Accumulating names of potential employers is easier today than ever, thanks to an ever-increasing number of directories and databases. But the blessing here is mixed. The sheer volume of information available today can be overwhelming, and unless you develop a system for gathering and organizing information, you run the risk of drowning in your own paperwork.

The best place to begin developing your list and setting up your system is the reference section of a local library, where you will find a variety of directories that offer basic information about thousands of companies across the United States. Among the directories you should be looking at initially are the following:

Million Dollar Directory, America's Leading Public and Private Companies. Lists roughly 160,000 moderate- to large-size public and private companies.

Standard & Poor's Register of Corporations, Directors and Executives. Although it lists fewer companies than the *Million Dollar Directory*, Standard & Poor's includes companies not listed there. It also offers biographical information on company executives.

George D. Hall Company Directories. A solid reference source of manufacturing and service companies. The directories in this series are regionalized.

The Directory of Corporate Affiliations. Lists about four thousand major companies, along with their subsidiaries and divisions—information not always available in other directories.

Corporate Technology Directory. Lists about thirty-five thousand manufacturing and high-tech companies.

In addition to the above directories, there are any number of industry-specific lists, local guides (Chamber of Commerce lists, for example), and association directories, some of which are easier to find than others. And here's a sobering statistic: The number of companies listed in all of these directories represents only a tiny fraction of the nearly eight and a half million businesses recognized by the Internal Revenue Service. All of which underscores, again, the importance of setting up a system.

One unusually well-organized job hunter we worked with long ago developed a simple system that could well serve as a model for you. He began by establishing basic criteria (industry, region, size, etc.), and then assigned each company he came across to one of three categories, based on those criteria he'd set up. Companies that met *all* the criteria became part of his A group; those that met most of the criteria became part of his B group; those that met only a few of the criteria became his C group. (Companies that didn't meet any of the criteria, of course, didn't get listed at all.)

You can develop any set of criteria you want, but the objective should be the same: not simply to amass a long list of companies, but to develop this list in an intelligent, systematic, and focused manner.

22

NETWORKING
Play the Numbers Game

THE BIGGEST MISTAKE MOST JOB HUNTERS MAKE when it comes to networking is not doing enough of it. The vast majority of jobs—as many as 80 percent by most estimates—are filled today by people who first heard about the opening informally, through another person. So no matter how many people become part of your network, it's never enough—not until one of the contacts leads to a job offer.

I'll go even further. Until you actually *have* a job, one of your chief goals each week should be to add people to your network. How many you add is up to you, but if you are not having success drumming up leads, ten new network contacts per week does not seem to me to be an unreasonable goal.

If adding a minimum of ten new people a week to your networking seems too ambitious a goal, consider this: Suppose you were to write down the names of ten people you would feel comfortable approaching for help in your job search. If you were to ask each of these ten people to give you three people *they* know, your original list of contacts would expand from ten to forty.

If you took the process one step further (that is, asked each new person for three names), your list would mushroom to 130 people. And that's from an original list of ten people, each of whom furnished only three names. If you can get your original list up to, say, twenty-five (and most people should be able to do this without any trouble), and you go through the same process, your list would exceed three hundred. That covers your quota (ten per week) for thirty weeks.

Networking takes time and effort. To do it effectively, you must get over the notion that by making people part of your job-search network, you are somehow "using" or "exploiting" them. Nonsense. Networking is an accepted practice in business today.

If you're uncomfortable approaching people, start with friends and family—the people with whom you feel most comfortable. Then gradually broaden the network to include acquaintances, former co-workers, former employers, former classmates, neighbors, customers, vendors, members of clubs and associations you belong to. The possibilities are all but endless.

Stay organized. The larger your network becomes, the more important it is to keep the names systematically organized. Use individual pages in a notebook or five- by eight-inch index cards for each name you get. Include for each entry all the basics: name, address, telephone number, company affiliation, and be sure to note how you made the connection. There should also be room on the card to keep track of when you speak to each person—even if it's for only a few seconds.

If you have access to a computer, consider setting up your network on a database. The big advantage of a database is that you can establish any number of cross-referencing criteria for each listing. That way, when a lead materializes in a particular company, you can go to your database, run a search based on that particular criterion, and in a matter of seconds find out which members of your network could help you make a connection in that company.

Once you have developed a good network, *use* it. If you have a specific need—the name of somebody in a particular company, for instance—get in touch with the two or three people in your network who might be willing to give you the information. Most people, and I cannot emphasize this point enough, will be happy to give you the information, assuming they have it, and assuming you ask for it in a direct and courteous way.

HOW TO SQUEEZE THE MOST OUT OF EACH NETWORK CONTACT

Y OU WILL RARELY HAVE MORE THAN ONE OPPORTUNITY to meet with or talk to most of the people who become part of your network. Make the most out of that conversation.

Your goal anytime you meet or converse with a network contact should be to come away with one or more of the following:

- A lead about an actual opening.
- A lead to a company that may be in the market for somebody with your background and skills.
- Names of other people with whom you might get in touch.
- Names of companies in which that person knows other people.

It is up to you to control the focus and tempo of the meeting or conversation. Once you've dispensed with the preliminaries, get right to the point. Present a concise overview of where you are in your job search. End the overview with what, specifically, you would like this person to do for you.

Are you looking for names in a particular company or industry? Ask for them. Are you looking for a way to meet a particular person in a company? Ask for it.

Any meeting or phone conversation you have with a new network contact will go more smoothly and will be more productive for you if you heed the following suggestions:

1. Let the person know, when you are setting up the meeting, what you expect to get out of the meeting, and make sure that your expectations are in line with what the person is able, and willing, to do.
2. Prepare your own *written* agenda for the meeting, based on what you want to gain from the conversation.
3. Determine at the beginning of the conversation (if it hasn't already been established) how much time the person can give you. Be considerate of your contact's time—be concise.
4. Take a supply of résumés with you.
5. Take careful notes, and if you are given names, don't be embarrassed to check on how they're spelled. The moment or two you fail to take during the meeting to double-check the spelling could cost you hours when the times comes to write a letter. (Suggestion: Don't ask for zip codes when you're getting names and addresses. The person won't know, and you can always get that information out of a directory.)
6. Don't confuse the goal of a networking conver-

sation or interview with the goal you might have
when you go to someone for general advice
about your career. Like most people, I am reluc-
tant to give out names of contacts when the
person seeking the contact seems unfocused. I
don't want to waste the time of the people whose
names I give.

SEEK OUT THE
WELL-CONNECTED

A GUIDING PRINCIPLE in your networking efforts
should be to seek out contacts who know the
most people. It might take a little more time and
ingenuity to locate these people and to arrange a
conversation with them. But the number of leads
you can get from *one* well-connected person will
exceed what you can get from a half-dozen others
whose contacts aren't as great.

It is commonly believed that the best-connected
people are the most powerful and best-known in
their fields. More often than not, though, the people
best equipped to give you names and leads are neither well-known nor powerful. They're simply people who thrive on making connections. And, by the
way, they are surprisingly approachable. As a rule,
they like being sought out because they take pride in
the connections they've developed.

One good way to get a fix on the best-connected

people in your particular area of interest is to get in touch with reporters who work for trade publications in that field. If you don't know any reporters personally, see if anyone on your network can make the connection.

Another good way to connect with the well-connected is to contact an organization (state or local professional association, for instance) made up of people in the industry you've targeted. Don't ask for the president. Ask for the program or membership chairman.

Here again, and at the risk of belaboring the point, I cannot overemphasize the importance of taking initiative. The worst thing that can happen if you call someone, introduce yourself, ask for a favor, and are turned down is simply that—someone turns you down. The chances of your being turned down, assuming you ask in a reasonable way, are a lot slimmer than you might think.

KEEP THE BALL IN YOUR COURT

WHENEVER ANYBODY AGREES TO DO SOMETHING on your behalf—make a call, arrange an interview, put in a good word for you—try to arrange it so that *you* are the one responsible for calling back to see if the task has been completed. By assuming this responsibility, you avoid the uncomfortable position of having to wait for somebody else to move off the dime before you can make a move yourself.

The people you approach may not want to go along with this arrangement and might insist that they get back to you. Don't force the issue, but don't give in too quickly, either. Asking someone to give you a general idea of when the two of you might talk again is not being pushy; it's being businesslike. As long as you are low-keyed and courteous, nobody is likely to get upset.

If the other person is willing to go along with your arrangement, set a reasonable deadline. Instead of asking, "Can I get back to you in a week or so?" suggest a specific day. ("I would like to get back to you on Monday in the early afternoon. Is that okay with you?")

Oh, yes. Make sure you call back when you say you are going to call back.

26

SHOW GRATITUDE

ALWAYS—ALWAYS!—SEND A FOLLOW-UP THANK-YOU note whenever anyone you've met for the first time agrees to do something for you that could help in your job search. Send it promptly. Make the sending of short thank-you notes (and they can be handwritten) to people who have given you leads or information a fixed part of your daily routine. If possible, include with the note something the person might value, such as a photocopy of an article that deals with a subject in which the person is interested.

The issue here goes beyond basic courtesy. I can think of several occasions in which receiving a nicely worded thank-you note has prodded me to follow up on a promise a little more quickly than I might have otherwise moved.

Should a suggestion or a name given you during an information interview lead to an actual interview, let the person who helped to arrange it know about it, with a short note or a phone call.

27

AIRBORNE
How to Get Job Leads by Mail

 RITING LETTERS AS A WAY TO *GENERATE* JOB leads (as opposed to following up on leads you have already generated) is a valid and proven job-search technique, but it is not a technique that lends itself equally well to all job searches, and not a technique that I would recommend without certain qualifications.

Letters whose purpose is to generate job leads can be divided roughly into four categories:

1. Individualized letters to people whose names you have obtained through your networking efforts.

2. Individualized letters to people you neither know nor have any entree to.

3. The same letter written to a group of specific people you don't know but who constitute a targeted audience.

4. A "broadcast" letter that goes out to a large group of people—not necessarily targeted—as part of a mass mailing.

There is no question about the strategic value of options one and two. Well-focused, solidly written letters targeted to key people will usually produce a response, and will often result in at least a phone conversation, if not an actual lead.

The debate over the value of these letters begins to heat up, however, whenever you leave the realm of letters targeted to specific individuals and move into the category of letter *campaigns*: a single letter sent to a large group of people.

Two issues predominate: One is cost; the other is logistics.

Large-scale mailings can get expensive. It isn't only the cost of postage. It's also the cost of stationery, envelopes, list procurement, not to mention the clerical work needed to produce the mailing.

Another problem is time. Even if you know how to use one of the print-merge features that comes with most word processors, you still need to figure out a way to get the names and addresses of all the companies and people you want to contact computed into the system.

Many outplacement companies discourage job seekers from embarking on large-scale mailings, but their reluctance to go this route often stems from their own budget constraints. Many outplacement agencies lack the resources to handle large-scale mailings.

My own feeling is that mailings *work*—but only if you are willing to take the time and effort that goes into developing a strong campaign: that is, a strong letter, a truly targeted list, and disciplined follow-up. When I say *work*, I mean this: You can generally count on a small percentage of responses.

The question you have to ask yourself when it comes to letter-writing campaigns is this: Are the time and expense that go into a large-scale mailing worth the relatively small return you can reasonably expect? It is certainly an option worth thinking about—if not an option you want to jump into before you have exhausted all other possibilities.

COLD CALLING
How to Shorten the Odds

COLD CALLING —calling companies at random to see if there are openings—is arguably the simplest of job-hunting strategies to pursue. All you need is a telephone, a pleasant voice, and a thick skin.

Cold calling, though, is rarely the most *productive* strategy to follow. It's tiring. It can be expensive. And it can be a punishing experience to anybody who doesn't handle rejection very well. This is why I hesitate to recommend the strategy—except for one thing: Every now and then, it pays off.

I heard not long ago about a Minneapolis woman who was making no headway with other job-lead techniques and decided one day to start calling companies cold. On the third morning, by the flukiest of flukes, she was connected to a manager whose assistant had announced an hour or so earlier that she was quitting. The woman did a good job of selling herself over the phone, making a joke about "fate." She went into an interview two mornings later. A week later, she was hired.

The odds of something like this happening to you on the twentieth cold call you make (or even on the one hundredth) are slightly better than your odds of winning the state lottery. But if you can afford the phone bills, if you have the energy and temperament that it takes to keep making calls, and if nothing else is working for you, cold calling is worth a try. Here are some suggestions that can help you tilt the odds in your favor.

1. Work from a Targeted List Before you do any cold calling, take some time to develop a reasonably targeted list—a list that includes *only* those companies that could conceivably be offering the kind of job you are looking for.

2. Try to Talk to a Decision Maker Your principal goal when you call any company cold is to get past the receptionist or central operator to talk directly with someone who has the power to hire you. *Who* that person is will depend on the size of the company and the kind of job you're looking for. But unless it's a very small company, chances are remote that a decision maker will be answering the phone.

If you don't have a specific name (see next

point), ask to be directed to the department (marketing, finance, etc.) you want to reach. If the person who answers wants to know why you're calling, don't be evasive: It won't work. The more evasive you are, the more suspicion you will provoke.

One final suggestion: Your chances of getting through to a decision maker are better if you call during those periods of the day when the phone of the person you are trying to reach isn't being covered by someone else. The most opportune times are early in the morning, after five, and during lunch hour.

3. Ask for a Hearing, Not a Job Should you succeed in getting someone on the phone who is willing to talk with you, don't ask for a *job* interview. That's an invitation to be cut short. Ask instead for the opportunity to simply come in and talk. By asking for help in general rather than making a specific interview request, you make it more difficult for the person to turn you down.

4. Never Leave a Message on a Machine or Voice Mail If you don't know the person you are trying to reach and you get connected to the person's voice mail or answering machine, don't leave a message. Leaving your name—and nothing else—on the answering machine of somebody you don't know is rude. Most people resent having to return a call to a person whose name they don't know, only to find that the person wants something from them. Keep calling until the person answers the phone.

GETTING BY THE GATEKEEPER

Your access to people you want to reach during your job search will often be blocked by gatekeepers—people whose job is to screen calls.

Gatekeepers can be receptionists, secretaries, assistants, and, in the case of small businesses, even spouses. Whoever they may be, they are forces you need to contend with and overcome in your job search.

There is no single proven way to get by a vigilant gatekeeper, but the one thing everyone agrees on is that you don't get very far by challenging the gatekeeper's authority. Nor does it pay to use deception—misrepresenting yourself so that your call can be forwarded—as a way of slipping by the gatekeeper.

Keep in mind your ultimate goal: not simply to make contact with somebody who might be able to hire you or help you, but to actually *get* the help or get hired. Granted, if you ultimately get hold of the person you're trying to reach by evading the gatekeeper, you might be admired for your ingenuity. Usually, though, the strategy backfires.

The best approach is to try to win gatekeepers over to your side. Here are three suggestions that might help:

1. Show gatekeepers the same respect and courtesy you intend to show the person you're trying to reach. Don't insult them by treating them as nonentities.

2. Find out the name of the gatekeeper the first time you call, and call the person by name when you make subsequent calls.

3. Be forthright. Let the gatekeeper know why you're calling, what you need, and what you hope to gain from the person the gatekeeper is trying to keep you from reaching.

CREATIVE READING
How to Get the Most Out of Want Ads

ANSWERING WANT ADS is dismissed by some career counselors as a waste of time. The reasoning is that only a small percentage of available jobs (about 10 percent by most estimates) ever actually appear in the classified ads, and those openings generally attract the largest number of applicants.

I agree with the general view that relying solely on classifieds is a mistake, but I also believe that ignoring such ads entirely is just as big a mistake.

Here are a few pointers about following classified ads that are especially worth keeping in mind:

1. Cast a Wide Net The most productive source of want ads is likely to be the Sunday edition of the major newspaper in your area, but don't stop there. Follow the classifieds in major trade publications in your field, and don't overlook national publications—regional editions of *The Wall Street Journal*, for instance—that list openings.

Another often overlooked source of classifieds—especially when it comes to openings in smaller companies—is suburban newspapers. If your local library doesn't subscribe to the newspapers published in neighboring communities, add the libraries in those areas to your research network. Ask friends in nearby communities to clip the classifieds from local newspapers and send them to you.

2. Read the Entire Section Don't limit your reading to the section relating solely to your job category. Read other sections, if for no other reason than to get some new ideas about companies that are hiring. If a company name is new to you, do some research; see if you can network your way into that office.

Remember, too, similar jobs listed by different companies often appear under different headings. Ads for computer programmers are sometimes listed under C, for *computer,* and sometimes under P, for *programmers.* Sales jobs in many papers are often listed under the industry heading and not under *Sales.*

3. Don't Expect a Reply and Don't Take It Personally Unless the qualifications you present in your résumé or cover letter are an almost perfect match to qualifications called for in the ad, your chances of being contacted for most jobs you apply for are not terribly good. In most, though not all cases, the typical ad for a good entry-level or mid-level job is likely to draw hundreds of responses, and somebody is going to screen the responses and pass on to decision makers only those résumés that match the specs of the ad.

This is not to say that you shouldn't respond to ads that interest you, and that you shouldn't take the

time to write as strong a cover letter as you can. Just
don't take it personally when you don't get a reply.
To increase your chances of getting a reply, use your
network to find someone in that company (assuming
you know the company's name) to hand-deliver your
résumé or put in an extra word for you.

One final observation: Some outplacement specialists recommend that you wait until several days
after an ad has appeared before sending in your response, the theory being that your response will get
a better reading if it is received after the initial flood
of responses has subsided. There may be some valid-
ity to this advice, but I can think of many situations
in which companies stopped looking at résumés once
they made the initial screening and identified a
group of candidates that seemed worth pursuing. On
the other hand, if in your research, you come across
an attractive job opportunity that was advertised
several weeks ago, don't assume the job has already
been filled or that the person hired for the job is
working out.

HOW TO BE HAPPILY RECRUITED

RECRUITERS PLAY AN IMPORTANT, if sometimes mis-
understood, role in the job market. Even in a
tight market, recruiters are still called upon by com-

panies of all sizes to find candidates for positions at all levels.

As chairman and CEO of a major personnel services firm, I hardly qualify as an objective observer, but let me offer, nonetheless, some thoughts on recruiters that you might find useful:

1. Recruiters as a group do not "find" jobs for you— not in the strict sense of the word. They simply try to match you to jobs they have been asked to fill. True, there is a great deal you can learn from an experienced recruiter about the job market and about positioning yourself in the market, but recruiters should not be confused with career counselors.

2. The differences among employment services or "agencies" and "search firms" and "head hunters" have more to do with the *level* of jobs they deal with than the basic service they provide. Employment agencies tend to specialize in lower-level jobs. Recruiters and search firms specialize in mid-level management positions. Individual search consultants tend to specialize in higher-salaried executive and senior management placements.

    Another difference, although one that has more relevance to the search professional than to the candidate, is that in many high-level searches, the search professional gets a retainer as opposed to getting paid when the candidate has been placed. (These differences notwithstanding, you should never pay a fee to any agency, search firm, or consultant. Fees should be paid by the client, not the candidate.)

3. If you plan to use recruiters as part of your job-

search strategy, look for agencies and search firms that specialize in your particular field or industry.

4. Employment firms as a general rule are easier to approach than search consultants or executive recruiters, but most search firms—particularly the smaller ones—will take a look at your résumé and cover letter when they arrive and will keep them on file. Getting search professionals who are not in the market for someone with your background to sit down and meet with you is extremely difficult to arrange—unless you know someone who can set up an interview for you.

5. Steer clear of any recruiter who does any of the following:

- Tries to sell you career-planning services (testing, résumé writing, etc.).
- Asks you to pay any fee (in the typical agency relationship, the fee is paid by the employer).
- Guarantees to find you a job.
- Tries to pressure you into taking a job you don't feel comfortable taking.

GET INVOLVED IN VOLUNTEER WORK

IF YOU WERE ACTIVE IN VOLUNTEER WORK before you began your job hunt, stay active. If you weren't involved in volunteer work before you began looking for a job, start doing it.

Approached intelligently and in the right spirit, getting actively involved with volunteer organizations helps your job-hunting efforts in several ways—quite apart from the personal reward you get from helping others and from contributing to the well-being of your community.

Practically speaking, the chief benefit you derive as a job hunter from getting involved with volunteer work is the opportunity it gives you to expand your network—all the more if the group or cause you work with puts you in touch with well-connected people in the local business community. The more responsibility you take on, the more likely you are to interact with the organization's board members, a significant proportion of whom are leaders in the local business community.

Volunteering can help your job search in another way as well. It gives you a chance to gain experience and develop skills that could make you a more attractive candidate. I heard recently of a stock analyst in Philadelphia who, through an active involvement with her local United Way, overcame what had long been one of her greatest weaknesses: her inability to get up in front of a group and make a convincing presentation. That newly developed skill, she insists, was the main reason she was hired by her current employer.

I recently learned, too, of a woman who, prior to getting involved with a fund-raising group in Florida, knew nothing about direct-mail solicitation. Her experience in developing and managing mailing lists helped her land a job with a small direct-marketing company whose chief clients are non-profit agencies.

Two points about volunteer work and its role in your job search bear special mention.

1. Be Strategic Everything else being equal, try to choose a cause that, in addition to doing good work for the community, does one of two things: puts you in direct contact with people likely to help you the most in your job search; gives you a chance to develop new skills.

2. Stay on Track As interested as you might get in the work, don't allow the time and effort you put into your volunteer work to detract from the time and effort you put into your job search.

BECOME A CELEBRITY

IN A MATTER OF SPEAKING, of course.

When I talk about "becoming a celebrity," I am talking mainly about increasing your visibility: making your name more familiar to a would-be employer than it might otherwise be.

This method of generating leads is probably the most difficult to pull off, and it doesn't lend itself to every job search. But if you can follow through on either of the two suggestions below, you will help your job-search efforts immeasurably.

1. **Write Articles** Getting articles published in major publications (*Harvard Business Review, The Wall Street Journal*) is tough, even for established writers. Not nearly as difficult as you may think, though, is publishing bylined articles in your local newspaper, in trade publications, or in association publications.

How *well* you write is less important in these situations than the quality and the timeliness of information you can offer readers. If your field is money management, for instance, you might want to talk to the editor of your local newspaper about an article on basic money management. If you are a computer specialist, your local newspaper might well be interested in an article on how to choose a personal computer or which software programs to buy.

The possibilities are endless. You simply have to look to your own background and expertise and try to come up with topics that would be of interest to the general public.

Once you have decided to get yourself into print, you have two choices. You can either write the piece and send it in to a publication you have targeted, or you can write a query letter to the editor of the publication, in which you describe the kind of article you would like to write and why you think it would be of interest to the readers of the publication.

To repeat, you don't have to be William Shakespeare to get these articles published. If your information is valid and useful, and if you can organize your ideas and write in a reasonably coherent style, the editors will smooth out the prose.

2. Give Talks Much of what I've said about writing articles applies to giving talks. You have to come up with ideas that not only showcase your expertise, but also give useful information to the average person.

There is no shortage of organizations for whom you might give such talks. There are women's groups, men's groups, school groups, industry groups, etc. It will take you a little bit of time to develop your first talk, but once you've presented your speech, you can pretty much repeat the same talk each time, customizing sections of it to each group. By the way, if you are going to pursue this strategy, make sure you have plenty of business "portrait" photographs and biographies to send to local papers.

MAKE TEMPING A PERMANENT STRATEGY

TEMPING IS A TERM that was once used exclusively in connection with lower-level administrative employees—receptionists, secretaries, clerks. Today, however, the picture is much different. The fastest growth segments in temporary employment today, in fact, are in the professional and technical professions.

The main reason that many companies today are relying more than ever on temporary employees, of course, is to maintain flexibility in a competitive marketplace. But here is a statistic that might surprise you. According to our studies, roughly one third of all temporary assignments become full-time positions.

It makes sense, doesn't it? Once you have worked for a while in a company and proven not only that can you do the job but that you can get along with everyone as well, you have an enormous advantage over other candidates who may not be familiar with the company.

Yet another good thing about temping is that it gives you a chance to meet new people, expand your network, and get a sense of how much you are likely to enjoy a particular job, a particular industry, or a particular company, should the possibility of a full-time job arise.

Here are a few points about temping that are especially worth bearing in mind:

Point number one is to take advantage of the growing number of agencies—Accountemps, for instance—that specialize in temping and, more important, specialize in your particular field. When you register with a professional temporary service, be sure to let them know what kind of assignments you prefer and how often you want to work. The more specific you are the better.

Point number two is to approach any temporary job you take as if, in fact, it was a full-time job—or, better still, as if your performance as a temp was the determining factor in whether you were hired. Most of the candidates I have known who were able to convert a temporary position into a full-time position were people who dedicated themselves wholeheartedly to the responsibilites of the temporary position. They didn't think of themselves as "temps" or even "consultants."

A third point is to view your temporary assignment as a chance to expand your network. Don't be hesitant about letting the people you're working with know that you're looking for full-time employment. And don't be shy, either, about asking your supervisor for an honest evaluation of your performance.

The final point worth stressing is to make sure that you keep the momentum going in your job search. It isn't that easy. If you have been working all day at a temporary job, the last thing you might feel like doing is to spend two or three hours that same day focusing on your job search. Somehow, though, you need to find the time and the energy to handle both jobs: your temporary job and the full-time job of finding a permanent job.

PART IV

INTERVIEWING AND BEYOND

Sixteen Ways to Win the Job You Want

☆

35

THE FOUR BIGGEST MYTHS ABOUT JOB INTERVIEWS

Myth 1: How you handle yourself during a job interview is the one thing, above all, that will determine whether or not you get the job.

Fact: The way you come across during an interview, important as it is, is only one of several factors that influence the hiring decision. More important in most cases is how closely your background and skills match the hiring criteria of the job under consideration. The chief challenge of a job interview therefore should not be so much to "sell yourself" but to sell the "fit" between what you have to offer and what the job for which you are being interviewed calls for.

Myth 2: The best way to prepare for a job interview is to anticipate the questions you are likely to be asked, and to memorize strategic answers.

Fact: The best way to prepare for a job interview is to find out as much as you can about the *company* and, if possible, about the person interviewing you. Having a general idea ahead of time of the questions you're likely to be asked and figuring out how you intend to answer those questions is helpful, but only to a point. If you *over*-prepare your answers are likely to sound "canned," and your credibility will suffer.

Myth 3: Most interviewers are good judges of character. You don't have to go out of your way to impress them.

Fact: Most people who conduct hiring interviews are notoriously weak in the skills it takes to get the proper information out of the people they interview. You can't expect them to elicit from you the information that will lead them to choose you over other candidates. You have to take upon yourself the responsibility of communicating key information in the interview.

Myth 4: You should never appear overeager during a job interview. If it looks as if you want the job too much, you lose your negotiating power.

Fact: This bit of advice is applicable in one situation only: when the company is actively recruiting you and you have other offers. Otherwise—and keep in mind the difference between being "eager" and "desperate"—you should not try to conceal the interest or excitement you feel about a particular job. I have never heard of anyone not being hired because he or she *wanted* the job—employers want candidates to be enthusiastic.

36

WHY YOU DON'T NEED TO BE AS NERVOUS AS YOU FEEL

To hear some people talk, you would think that handling yourself effectively during a job interview required a set of highly complex and esoteric skills that are unique to job interviewing.

This simply is not true. Most of the "skills" you need to come across well in a job interview are basic people-to-people skills: the ability to pay attention, to listen, and, most important, to show genuine and enthusiastic interest in what the other person is saying.

The reason I emphasize this point is that too many job books depict job interviews as Kafkaesque chess matches, in which every question is designed to elicit a response with a hidden meaning, and every answer is designed to create an impression that goes beyond what is actually being said.

I don't deny that there is a certain element of game playing in most interview situations and that certain influence techniques do, in fact, work.

In general, though, candidates who come across well in job interviews are *not* skilled game players: they're solid candidates. They come to interviews well prepared. They project a positive attitude. They're not afraid to be themselves.

I don't mean to suggerst here that you can't learn, practice, and improve upon certain skills that will enhance your ability to make a favorable impression.

Just bear in mind that the most important interviewing skill is something you're probably good at already: being yourself.

HOMEWORK
The Ultimate Competitive Edge

Y OU CAN NEVER KNOW TOO MUCH about the company interviewing you—or about the person conducting the interview. Here is a case in point.

Mary Ann is a marketing specialist who was one of three finalists for a job in the marketing department of a major bank. One reason she became a finalist in the first place is that she had spent nearly a week in the library making photocopies of all the newspaper ads the bank had been running for the past three years, thus enabling her to discuss specific marketing strategies as though she had actually been with the bank when the ads were written.

Even so, she felt the need to do more. In one of her interviews, someone mentioned the name of the man who had headed the bank's marketing department for more than fifteen years. Mary Ann didn't know the man, who had since retired and was now living in South Carolina, but she managed to get his number through telephone directory assistance. She called him, explained her situation, and asked if he would give her some advice on what she might do to enhance her chances of getting the job.

The ex-marketing director not only agreed to help Mary Ann—he was remarkably candid. Among other things, he told her that the woman now heading the department was a "detail fanatic." Armed with this information, Mary Ann went out of her way during her interview to be highly specific in her answers. She got the job.

Listed below are some of the things to find out before going to an interview. You may not be able to gather *all* the information you need to gain this knowledge, but do your best to find out:

- What product or service the company sells and how it sells it.
- About the company's reputation in the industry.
- About the company's corporate culture (assuming it is large enough to have a corporate culture).
- What important trends are currently taking place in the company's industry.
- Who are the company's most formidable competitors.
- About any recent deals that have been made involving the company or the industry in general.
- Who are the company's key executives.

Some places to look for this information:

1. The company's own literature: its annual report, ads, employee publications, newsletters, promotional brochures. If the company is publicly traded and it files annual quarterly reports with the Securities and Exchange Commission, you can get copies of the most recent reports through the SEC.

2. Articles about the company that may have appeared in newspapers and magazines within the last few years. (Check the *Reader's Guide to Periodicals* or the *Business Periodicals Index* in your library, or find a library that has computer search capability. But keep in mind that not all magazines are listed in these places.)
3. Books that contain descriptions of the company. (Example: *The 100 Best Companies to Work For*.)
4. Directory listings.
5. Research reports from brokerage houses.

And if you want to go even further:

Search out people currently or recently employed by the company. Talk to people who either sell or buy from the company. Talk to the company's competitors.

How do you get in touch with these people? By digging, by being aggressive, and by using your network. It's trench warfare, but it pays off.

38

DON'T SHOOT YOURSELF IN THE FOOT

IN A JOB MARKET as competitive as today's, the last thing you can afford is to make silly mistakes. Most of the suggestions listed below fall under the category of common sense. All are worth thinking about.

1. Call Ahead to Confirm the Appointment
Calling ahead to confirm an appointment accomplishes two things: It eliminates the possibility, however remote, that you and the person interviewing you got your signals mixed when setting the time and date; it sends a message to the interviewer that you are someone who pays attention to details.

2. Dress Appropriately The rule of thumb when dressing for a job interview is to play it safe. Your goal, as I've already said, is to look professional, not to make a splashy fashion statement; to blend in, not stand out.

3. Arrive Early Always give yourself *more* time than you actually need to arrive at an interview on time, and take into account any contingency—heavy traffic, for instance—that could affect your arrival time. If the interview is in a part of town you're unfamiliar with, make sure you know how to get there—even if it means driving there the day before. Should you arrive well ahead of schedule, use the extra time to relax, collect your thoughts, and give yourself a final once-over in the bathroom. Plan to show up at the interviewer's office about five minutes before the interview is scheduled to begin.

4. Arrive Alone Never bring anybody with you to a job interview. If someone has come along for the ride or has given you a ride, have the person wait outside.

5. Watch Your Reception Etiquette Don't do anything while you're waiting in the reception room that might draw attention. Keep in mind that you are being evaluated from the moment you enter the lobby. More often than you might think, reception-ists comment on the comportment of candidates to people in the company who have a hand in making hiring decisions. Especially taboo are the following behaviors:

> Applying cosmetics
>
> Smoking or eating
>
> Listening to a personal stereo
>
> Using a cellular phone
>
> Reading any book or magazine whose subject might be controversial to the average person
>
> Any nervous mannerisms (humming, drumming your fingers against a table, pacing)

6. Don't Offer Opinions on Sensitive Subjects Sensitive subjects—and I include in this category religion, politics, and sex—don't usually come up in a job interview. But if they do, keep your opinions to yourself.

7. Don't Criticize Former Employers Even if you think you have been given license to do so (the interviewer volunteers a negative remark, for in-stance), never say anything even remotely negative about the company or people for whom you worked.

8. Don't Talk About Your Problems Even if the interviewer invites you to talk about how tough things are in the job market, don't allow the inter-view to turn into a therapy session. You are not looking for sympathy. You are looking for an offer. Be upbeat.

9. Don't Name-drop Mentioning important people you know or have worked with is okay as long as the mention is relevant to your background. Otherwise, don't do it. It turns most people off.

ALWAYS PLAY TO WIN

G O INTO EVERY INTERVIEW with one objective, above all: to get an offer.

The job for which you are being interviewed might not seem exciting to you. You may not be thrilled about the company. You may have dozens of other irons in the fire. It doesn't matter. Go for it, anyway.

Here are four reasons why it is so important to treat every interview as if the job at stake were your dream job, regardless of how excited you are about the job itself:

1. You always have the option, if indeed you are offered the job, to turn it down, or, who knows, to modify it so that it is more appealing to you.
2. Simply being offered a job, regardless of whether you take it, helps your morale and self-esteem. It gives you more confidence when you are interviewed for a job you care about.
3. If you go into an interview with anything less than a "I want this job" attitude, your perfor-

mance will usually be lackluster, and the negative impression you leave on the interviewer
could come back to haunt you. The interviewer
might know other people in the field and could,
in some way, squelch your chances of getting a
different job.

4. An interviewer sufficiently impressed with you
to offer a job you turn down is likely to recommend you to someone else, as long as you have
been gracious.

FIND COMMON GROUND WITH YOUR INTERVIEWER

M OST OF WHAT WE HAVE ALWAYS BEEN TOLD about the
importance of first impressions turns out to be
true, according to most psychological reports on the
subject. What holds true for first impressions in general holds equally true for job interviews. The impression you make in the first moment or two of a
job interview does indeed have a significant impact
on the overall impression you leave behind. And
while it is certainly possible to overcome the effects
of an unfavorable first impression, it is not easy.

The basics of making a good first impression are
fairly obvious, so I will cover them only briefly. Of
course, you should be appropriately and neatly
dressed and well groomed—that's a given. You also
should be aware of your posture (erect, but relaxed).

Make sure, too, that when you greet the interviewer, you do so with good eye contact, with a firm (but not crushing) handshake, and with a smile.

Assuming these basics are taken care of, the best advice I can give you about making a favorable first impression is to try to build rapport by finding common ground—that is, a topic of conversation that can get the interview off to a relaxing start. An experienced interviewer will try to do this by making mention of the weather or by asking a simple question such as, "Did you have any trouble finding the place?" Even so, it's a good idea for you to get the conversation started on a subject that *you* feel comfortable talking about.

Be observant as you enter the office. Be on the lookout for anything—the view, the style of the desk, photographs or paintings on the wall—interesting or unusual enough to mention as a way to break the ice. If you can do this, you accomplish two things: One, you make yourself more relaxed; two, you put your interviewer in a more receptive frame of mind.

KNOW WHAT'S COMING
Thirteen Questions You Should Be Prepared to Answer No Matter What

MOST PEOPLE WHO CONDUCT JOB INTERVIEWS ask pretty much the same questions, and so there is no excuse for not being able to give good answers to most of the questions you are likely to be asked. You need to be careful, however, that your answers do not sound too pat. Otherwise, you lose credibility.

Listed below are thirteen of the questions that are the most likely to be asked at job interviews, along with some guidelines on how to answer them. Give some thought to how you will answer these questions, and, as you go on interviews, add to the list any questions that come up for the first time. I see nothing wrong with practicing these answers aloud when you're relaxing at home or driving in your car, but, again, don't try to memorize the answers.

1. Tell me a little about yourself?

Comment: Keep your answer brief. Don't hesitate to ask the interviewer to narrow the scope of the question.

2. What did you do in your last job?

Comment: Focus on key responsibilities. Tailor the answer to what you perceive to be the main requirements of the job you're seeking.

3. What do you think you can offer our company?

Comment: Use the question as an opportunity to elaborate on what you know about the company, based on the homework you have done.

4. What do you want to be doing in five years?

Comment: You don't have to be too specific when you answer this—but don't be afraid to aim high.

5. Why did you leave your last job?

Comment: Be honest. If you were fired, say so, but be prepared to offer a reasonable explanation.

6. From what you have seen, what do you think of our company?

Comment: A not-too-smart question frequently asked by inexperienced interviewers. Show enthusiasm. Never criticize.

7. What were your best subjects in school?

Comment: A frequently asked question during entry-level job interviews. Be honest, but bear in mind that the interviewer might be trying to connect the subjects you were good at with the job requirements.

8. What tasks do you find the most boring?

Comment: A good question that trips up a lot of people. What an interviewer might be looking for with this question are some insights into your personality. It's okay to be general in your response.

9. What do you consider your greatest strengths?

Comment: As long as you don't go overboard, don't hesitate to toot your own horn. Strengthen your claims by giving illustrations of how a particular strength translated into a specific accomplishment at your last job.

10. What do you consider your biggest weaknesses?

Comment: A no-win question. Nobody expects you to admit worst faults. Be prepared to throw in a few harmless weaknesses—"I get a little tunneled sometimes,"—along with what you are doing to strengthen those weaknesses.

11. What are your salary expectations?

Comment: Try to finesse this question, couching it in terms of the job and the opportunity. If pressed, offer a range and don't be afraid to err on the high side. Stress your desire to earn top pay for the position, but only in return for top performance.

12. What are the three most recent books you have read?

Comment: If you can't offer a good answer to this question, it's your own fault. Be better prepared the next time. Try to include in your answer at least *one* book that is related to either the job you're interviewing for or self-improvement in general.

13. What do you like to do in your spare time?

Comment: Whatever you say, show enthusiasm.

42

SELLING THE "FIT"
The Three Things, Above All, You Should Bear in Mind When You Are Answering Questions

WHILE THE NUMBER OF QUESTIONS asked during an interview might be in the dozens, the number of questions interviewers will be asking themselves about you is far more finite.

Essentially, there are three questions whose answers will determine whether you get an offer:

1. Can you do the job?
2. Will you fit in?
3. Will you be motivated to do a good job?

These questions are extremely useful to keep in mind as you prepare for each interview. One way or the other, your answers to any question you are asked should be keyed to these three questions. Why? Because that is what your interviewer will do.

THE CARE AND FEEDING OF INEXPERIENCED INTERVIEWERS

EVERYTHING ELSE BEING EQUAL, you are better off being interviewed by a tough-nosed hiring professional—somebody who doesn't hesitate to ask difficult questions or to probe—than you are being interviewed by someone who has no idea what questions to ask and how to evaluate the answers.

Here's why. With experienced interviewers, you can usually assume that if you don't get an offer, it will be for the right reason: You simply were not as qualified as other candidates. With inexperienced interviewers, you run the risk of losing out not because you weren't qualified but because your qualifications never got communicated during the interview.

You can generally sense early on in the meeting how experienced your interviewer is. Experienced interviewers are usually well prepared when you enter the office. The seating arrangements have already been set up; your résumé is usually sitting on the top of the desk; and steps have been taken to make sure the two of your aren't interrupted.

Usually, too, an experienced interviewer will have prepared the questions ahead of time and will be taking notes as you give your answers.

If you begin to suspect that your interviewer is clearly not in control of the process, here's what to do:

1. Don't allow the frazzled atmosphere that often prevails in a disorganized interview dull your own sense of purpose. Stick to your plan.
2. Whenever you are given an opening, steer the interviewer toward those topics that will showcase your strengths.
3. Don't do or say anything that might be interpreted as criticism for how the interview is going. If you feel interview conditions are preventing you from presenting your story, see if you can arrange for another interview. If the person seems unusually distracted, you might suggest that you come at the end of the day or first thing the next morning. Just be as tactful as you can.

OF COURSE I WAS LISTENING, COULDN'T YOU HEAR ME?

THE FOLLOWING STORY WAS RELAYED TO ME not long ago by the president of a small but successful public relations firm in New York. It illustrates how critical it is during a job interview to be an active, *aggressive* listener.

The firm was in the market for someone to work on a new account—a food company whose president was infamous for his ferocious temper and demanding, difficult personality. So, in addition to the job's basic qualifications—that the candidate have good media relations and strong writing skills—the PR firm's president was concerned about personality. He wanted somebody with an easygoing and flexible temperament—somebody who knew how to handle difficult people.

One of the leading candidates for the job was a man whose writing and media skills were clearly stronger than those of anybody else being considered. So the only thing the candidate had to demonstrate during his interview was that he had an easygoing personality.

That did not happen. Several times during the interview, the president of the PR firm stressed that while he was impressed with the candidate's media contacts and writing ability, his chief concern was that the client was difficult and he wanted to make sure there wouldn't be any personality conflicts.

The candidate wasn't listening. Over and over, he kept stressing how good a writer he was and how good he was at working with the press. He never got the message about how important personality was, and he never got hired.

You may think this is an extreme example, but it is an almost inevitable occurrence if you fail to focus the full measure of your attention on what the person on the other side of the desk is saying to you. It's also an inevitable occurrence if you are so focused on *your* agenda—what you want to say—that you fail to pay attention to what your interviewer needs to *hear*, if you are to get the offer.

PREEMPTIVE STRIKE
How to Bring Objections to the Surface

MOST PEOPLE WHO MAKE HIRING DECISIONS ARE RISK-AVERSIVE, more likely to be scared away by what they see as your "negatives" than they are to be drawn to you because of your strengths. One way or the other, you need to work this principle into your interviewing strategy.

A "negative" is anything about you or your background that might give the interviewer reason to think that you can't do the job, that you won't fit in, or that you won't be motivated to hang in there for the long run.

Certain "negatives" are logical—even obvious. Example: Your background does not include experience that relates *directly* to the responsibilities of the job under consideration.

But "negatives" can also be arbitrary and, in some cases, blatantly prejudicial.

Regrettably, there isn't too much you can do if the person interviewing is, in fact, making prejudicial evaluations—just as long as the person doesn't ask questions that could be interpreted as having a bias.

Other objections, however, are different and can often be defused if you know how to bring them to the surface. If you know for a fact, for instance, that you are overqualified for a job you want, I see nothing wrong with saying, "Look, I know my résumé might make me seem overqualified, but . . ." and then present your reason why that concern shouldn't worry the interviewer.

But let me offer this caveat: Don't jump the gun. Be reasonably certain—before you bring an objection to the surface—that the objection exists.

Once you bring the objection to the surface, the best way to defuse it is to address the concern *behind* the objection rather than the objection itself. To accomplish this, you might have to do some probing.

Example: An interviewer mentions the fact that your experience has been limited to small firms, whereas the job under consideration is with a large firm. What you don't know here is what, specifically, the interviewer is worried about. It could be that you're not a team player, or that you're too entrepreneurial. You have no way of knowing which concern has prompted the question—which is why you need to ask.

Once you have an answer, frame your response accordingly. If the interviewer brings up the issue of "team playing," you might want to point out that your former company did, in fact, operate as a team. If the concern is that as an entrepreneur, you might not be willing to deal with the bureaucracy of a large company, you might point out that even though you were part of a small company, you had to deal with bureaucracies in the companies that were your customers.

SWITCHING HATS
What to Do When You're Invited to Ask Questions

Y OU WILL ALMOST ALWAYS HAVE A CHANCE in a job interview to ask questions, and the *kinds* of questions you ask will obviously have a bearing on the impression you make. Some people advise candidates to draw up a list of questions ahead of time—not necessarily because you want these questions answered but because you want to impress the interviewer.

As you probably have gathered by now, I do not advocate using manipulative devices in interviews—mainly because most people are able to see through them. I do, however, believe that you should ask substantive, intelligent questions—questions that relate to the position and, in particular, the expectations of the employer.

It's also important to keep in mind questions that you *shouldn't* ask in the initial interview. Questions I place in this category include:

- How long is the average workday?
- Vacations and days off
- Specifics about benefits
- Smoking breaks

TRUTH OR CONSEQUENCES
How to Handle Questions You Would Rather Not Answer

I KNOW A PERSONNEL EXECUTIVE who has a trick question he asks nearly every candidate he interviews. Whenever the candidate mentions a company or organization with which he or she has been involved, the personnel executive responds by saying, "Oh, then you must know George Hale."

There is no George Hale. Yet, rather than admit that they do not know someone as obviously important as George Hale, some candidates will say something such as, "I think I may have met him once or twice." These candidates, fairly or unfairly, rarely make the final cut.

While I don't approve of these tactics, there is a lesson to be learned from them. Whenever you are in a situation in which giving a truthful answer could, in your view, hurt your chances of being hired, take the risk and tell the truth. Embarrassing or damaging as the truth may seem, you still have the opportunity to offer an answer and, by doing so, contain the damage. Get caught in a lie, regardless of how inconsequential that lie may be, and everything else you've said immediately comes under suspicion. I believe that it is to your advantage to maintain the highest ethical standards in your job search at all times.

This principle applies to even mild bending of the truth—for instance, letting on that you know someone (like George Hale) or something that you really don't know. As Mark McCormack points out in *What They Don't Teach You in Harvard Business School,* "Not admitting what you don't know can lead to suspicion about what you do know."

Let me add three corollaries to the principle I've just described:

1. Telling the truth is not the same thing as volunteering information you haven't been asked to volunteer. And *not* volunteering that information is not the same thing as lying. If there are aspects of your background that might hurt your chances, and the conversation never gets around to those aspects, consider yourself lucky. Don't tempt fate.

2. Don't *over*-answer questions, or steer answers into areas you'd rather not talk about. The lone exception to this principle is when you have good reason to believe that the interviewer already knows about some problems you may have had, and you feel it is in your best interest to bring these issues to the surface.

3. Be prepared to offer a reasonable explanation for any aspects of your background that might work

against you should they emerge in the discussion. If you were fired from your last job for a specific reason, for instance, make sure you can explain what happened and can offer some assurances that it won't happen again. Incidentally, there is nothing wrong with simply admitting, "I made a mistake," if that is the case.

ALWAYS WALK AWAY WITH SOMETHING

A JOB INTERVIEW THAT DOESN'T RESULT IN A JOB OFFER is neither a failure nor a waste of your time—not if you can walk away with something you can use to enhance your chance of success the next time around.

That "something" might be a lead to other companies or names of other people who could become part of your ongoing networking. It could also be something less tangible but still valuable—added insights about you, your job campaign strategy, or the way you handled yourself in the interview.

You need to be careful about when, and how, you get this information. Or, to put the same thought another way, don't be in a hurry to bail out of a plane that isn't necessarily in trouble. As long as you feel you are in the running for the job, keep the interview focused on the job at hand.

Frequently, though, you can tell early on in an interview that the fit just isn't there: that what the company is looking for, you can't really offer. In this situation, it makes good sense to shift the focus away from the job at hand and focus instead on your job search in general. Chances are, the person who interviews you will welcome the shift. Nobody is comfortable in a situation in which one or both persons are simply going through the motions.

I see nothing wrong, either, with trying to find out—as the interview is about to wind up—if you are, in fact, a serious candidate for the job. Be careful, though, about how you ask the question. Instead of personalizing the question ("Do I have a chance for this job?"), you are better off asking the same question indirectly ("Have you interviewed a lot of good people for this job?").

One way you can tell if you are still in the running is by paying attention to the *kinds* of questions you're asked as the meeting draws to a close. If you're asked specific questions about your availability, it's a good, although not certain, sign that you've met the basic qualifications.

How candid an answer you get to questions regarding how serious a candidate you are will depend on the interviewer, on the rapport you have established, and, in particular, on how the person interprets your question.

If you ask the question in a way that makes you seem desperate and vulnerable, you're probably going to get a polite but noncommittal answer—something along the lines of, "Well, you have some good qualifications, but we have other people we want to talk to." If your interviewer sincerely believes you are looking for feedback and not simply encouragement, the next few moments of the meeting could be quite valuable.

A bolder and somewhat riskier strategy is to come right out and ask for the help. You say something like, "I get the feeling that I'm not really the right person for this job. But maybe you can give me some help." I recommend this latter strategy in only two situations: one, when you are sure that even if the job were to be offered to you, you would turn it down; two, when you are absolutely sure that you're out of the running.

MAKE A GOOD LAST IMPRESSION

WHATEVER ELSE YOU DO in the final moments of your interview, and regardless of how the interview went, make sure you do the following:

1. Express your gratitude to the interviewer for the opportunity you have been given—no matter how the interview went.
2. Find out if there is anything else you might do (send in additional samples of your work?) that might give the interviewer a better sense of what you can contribute.
3. Let the interviewer know (assuming you're being genuine) that you are extremely interested in the position.
4. Let the interviewer know that you believe you can handle the job and make a contribution.

5. Regardless of how it went or where you left
    things at the end, follow every interview with a
    letter or short note. Keep it brief, and make sure
    you do the following things:

*   Thank the interviewer for the time he or she
    gave you and mention specifically anything ex-
    tra that person may have done for you, such as
    giving you some names.
*   Reaffirm your interest in the position.
*   Recap the key reasons why you are qualified for
    the job.
*   Reiterate the commitment you made at the end
    of the interview.

Your follow-up letter shouldn't run more than a
page. Triple-check it for typos, and make sure you've
spelled all the names correctly.

50

SPIN CONTROL
Managing Your References

NEVER ASSUME THAT THE PEOPLE WHOSE NAMES YOU'VE
GIVEN as references will say what you would like
them to say, and never assume that people whose
names you *haven't* given as references won't be approached by a company interested in hiring you. In
short, don't take references for granted. Keep in
mind that once a company is checking your refer-

ences, you can pretty much assume that it is interested in hiring you, and what the person seeking the reference wants is to *verify* information you have already given them.

The references you get, in other words, do not have to "sell" you to the company. You simply need to make sure that the person giving the reference doesn't say anything, inadvertently or not, that creates doubt or knocks you out of the running altogether. Here are four guidelines:

1. Never list your references on either your résumé or on a cover letter. Always wait until you have been asked to supply them.

2. Never give as a reference anyone you haven't spoken to first and anyone who hasn't agreed to talk to a potential employer on your behalf.

3. Make sure that at least one of the people you list as a reference is someone you worked for in your most recent job. If you left on bad terms, go back and talk to that person so that you can agree upon a mutually acceptable reason for leaving. Otherwise, let the interviewer know that your former company might not have nice things to say about you, and be prepared to explain why.

4. Once you know that the company is checking on your references, get in touch with the people and fill them in, as much as possible, on the job you are being considered for and what specific qualities you think the company is concerned about.

5. If you have good reason to believe that your former employer, when approached for reference information, will not have flattering things to say about you, alert the interviewer to the pos-

sibility. It isn't necessary to go into great detail about what happened. Dismiss it as a personality clash and let it go at that. Keep in mind, however, that this strategy will work when you have only *one* potentially bad reference to worry about.

Epilogue
Prepare for Next Time

IT IS HARDLY A SECRET THAT JOB SECURITY, in the comforting, old-fashioned sense of the term, is a thing of the past. Even if you are hired for a job you are good at and enjoy, and even if the company that hires you is doing well and has a reputation for "looking after its people," you can no longer take your job for granted. No one today is bulletproof.

Today, more than ever, you need to approach your job in terms of what Robert Half, our company's original founder, calls "career insurance."

"Career insurance" can best be defined as steps you take, *while you're still employed* to make sure that: one, you are less vulnerable than others in your company when and if cutbacks occur; and, two, you are already prepared for a job search if indeed the ax falls again.

Among the specific steps you can be taking to give yourself this advantage are the following:

Stay Current Even if there is no *practical* need for it in your current job, keep pace with new developments in your field. Be sure you subscribe to—and read—the key trade publications in your business. Keep a file of articles and reports that focus on what's new and important. If your schedule permits, go to seminars that cover new trends and developments, and try to attend at least one major conference or convention in your field each year.

Broaden Your Responsibilities If the job description of your new position is narrow and technically bound, look for ways—seminars and courses, for instance—to broaden it with skills and responsibilities that will make you more marketable down the road. Especially important in today's job market, as you should know by now, are communication skills, being a team player, and having the ability to complete tasks with little supervision when necessary.

Keep an Ongoing Record of Your Accomplishments Start accumulating a file of your accomplishments. The file should include letters of commendation, favorable appraisals, and any decision or suggestions you have made that produced bottom-line results. Such a file is indispensable when the time comes to put together a résumé. It could also come in handy if you find yourself in a severance negotiation.

Stay in Contact with Recruiters Regardless of how secure you may feel in your new job, stay in touch with any recruiters you got to know during your search. If you are approached by a recruiter or search consultant who wants to talk about a possible job, don't let the fact that you are just settling into a new job keep you from maintaining the relationship.

Keep Your Network Alive Don't allow the network you cultivated during your job search to dry up.

Stay in touch with the people who were the most helpful. Keep adding new people.

Develop a "Résumé-in-Waiting" Writing a new résumé shortly after you have taken a new job might strike you as the same thing as writing your own obituary, but it's a good idea, anyway. One of the first things you need when you begin looking for a job is a résumé. Having one ready (or at least in progress) will get you out of the starting block that much sooner.

Be Helpful to Others When people looking for help in their own job searches call you for contacts or information, be as helpful and considerate as you can. You never know when you'll need them to return the favor.

ABOUT THE AUTHOR

Harold M. "Max" Messmer, Jr., is chairman and chief executive officer of Robert Half International Inc., the world's largest specialized staffing firm. The New York Stock Exchange–listed company has four major divisions for temporary and permanent placement: Accountemps® and Robert Half®, for accounting, finance and information technology specialists; OfficeTeam®, for administrative and office professionals; and The Affiliates®, for legal personnel.

Mr. Messmer serves on the boards of directors of several New York Stock Exchange–listed companies, including Airborne Freight Corporation; Pacific Enterprises, parent company of Southern California Gas Company; and Health Care Property Investors, Inc. He is also a board member of NationsBank of North Carolina, N.A., and Spieker Properties, Inc. From 1985 to 1988, Mr. Messmer served on the President's Advisory Committee on Trade Negotiations.

Mr. Messmer has written numerous articles on hiring and staffing for a variety of professional publications. He is also the author of *Staffing Europe: An Indispensable Guide to Hiring and Being Hired in the New Europe*, published in 1991.

A summa cum laude graduate of Loyola University, Mr. Messmer holds a law degree from the New York University School of Law.